PULL UP A SANDBAG

Third edition
published in 2011 by

WOODFIELD PUBLISHING LTD
Bognor Regis ~ West Sussex ~ England ~ PO21 5EL
www.woodfieldpublishing.co.uk

ISBN 1-84683-074-5

PULL UP A SANDBAG

Jokes & Anecdotes Contributed by British Military Personnel

COMPILED BY
JONATHAN SMILES

Woodfield

Woodfield Publishing Ltd

Woodfield House ~ Babsham Lane ~ Bognor Regis ~ West Sussex ~ PO21 5EL
telephone 01243 821234 ~ **e-mail** enquiries@woodfieldpublishing.co.uk

Interesting and informative books on a variety of subjects

For full details of all our published titles, visit our website at
www.woodfieldpublishing.co.uk

~ Contents ~

Our contribution to
Help for Heroes

The collaborators on this book are former soldiers who have lost friends and seen others injured while on operations and recognise that they themselves have been fortunate to come through their years of military service unscathed.

In addition to entertaining our fellow soldiers, we wanted this book to raise funds for a suitable charity.

Many worthwhile charities and organisations continue to help British service personnel and their families affected by conflict, so the choice of which to support was difficult, but the final decision was agreed wholeheartedly.

Help for Heroes was singled out for its combination of efficiency and transparency. They ensure that 97% of all donations go towards helping serving and former military personnel wounded on operations. H4H also outline exactly how much has been donated, where and how donations will be used, and include estimated timeframes.

Our heartfelt thanks go to all who are involved with Help for Heroes, whether as members of staff or donors.

Our publishers, Woodfield Publishing Ltd, have kindly agreed to donate £1 from the sale of every copy of *Pull Up a Sandbag* to Help for Heroes.

We hope to raise a significant sum.

Thank you for your support!

About *Help for Heroes*

HELP *for*
HEROES
Support for our Wounded

"What is H4H all about? It's about the blokes, our men and women. It's about Derri, a rugby player who has lost both his legs, it's about Carl whose jaw is wired up so he has been drinking through a straw. It's about Richard who was handed a mobile phone as he lay on the stretcher so he could say goodbye to his wife. It is about Ben, it's about Steven and Andy and Mark, it's about them all. They are just blokes but they are our blokes; they are our heroes. We want to help our heroes."

The charity **Help for Heroes** was launched in October 2007 in response to the desire of ordinary people to do something practical to help our wounded servicemen and women. As individuals we are powerless to prevent war and we feel helpless that we are unable to stop our men and women from being killed and wounded. By joining together as Help for Heroes, we are doing something practical to help; we are doing our bit.

Help for Heroes is very simple; we are strictly non-political, we recognize that wars happen under any government, and we are non-critical, preferring to get on with the job rather than talking about rights and wrongs.

Our first task, given to us by General Sir Richard Dannatt, the Head of the Army, was to raise £6 million to help provide a swimming pool and gym complex at the tri service rehabilitation centre at Headley Court. With the support of Royalty, The Armed Forces, Celebrities, the Press and thousands of ordinary, decent people, we achieved that target in our first eight months.

Our first task may be complete, but our job is not and, while our young men and women continue to be wounded, we intend to be there to help. We are pushing on with even more determination, buoyed by the extraordinary support of the public in our first few months, to ensure that the wounded get the best help, support and futures that they deserve.

Our Servicemen and women give more, risk more and sacrifice more, so we believe that they should be given more; we believe they deserve the very best. They say they are not Heroes, that they are just blokes doing their job; we say that anyone who volunteers to join the Armed Forces and serve in time of war is a hero and we want to help our heroes.

Bryn Parry
*Appeal Chairman & Co Founder of **Help for Heroes***
quoted from **www.helpforheroes.co.uk**

It is a good thing for an uneducated man to read books of quotations... The quotations, when engraved upon the memory, give you good thoughts. They also make you anxious to read the authors and look for more.

Winston Churchill

It should be an amusing thing to read Pull Up a Sandbag, but accept it as no more than light entertainment...
The stories, if engraved upon the mind, give perverse thoughts and may constitute permanent mental damage. On the other hand, anxiety to read the authors and look for more should be regarded as beneficial.

Jonathan Smiles

Introduction

For it's Tommy this, an' Tommy that, an' "Chuck him out, the brute!"
But it's "Saviour of 'is country" when the guns begin to shoot;
Rudyard Kipling, 1890

Soldiers are different. Ask any civilian. Ask any soldier, for that matter, and he will agree, but you will get a different set of reasons. That said, the one characteristic they are both likely to include is the sense of humour. Military humour is usually irreverent, often black, sometimes basic or obscene, and gives little or no thought to being politically correct. At its core is the essential ingredient for any true sense of humour, the ability to laugh at oneself. RSMs, OCs and COs are constitutionally entitled to suppress this last ingredient, but it's still in there, believe me!

This compilation includes examples of all the above. The stories are based on actual events and are as true as any story remains after the embellishments of successive raconteurs, and as accurate as recollection can be after memory survives the passing years and occasional alcohol-based filtration.

The idea behind this book is neither new nor original. The seeds were sown over ten years ago, but lay dormant while its authors got on with the delights of military service and eventual transition to civilian life, in the process living through many of the more recent stories. Life as ex-squaddies brought little change, with subsequent 'tours' taking in Bosnia, Kosovo, Afghanistan and Iraq, as well as parts of North Africa and South East Asia. The seeds germinated during the summer of 2008, thanks to the warmth of Sarajevo sunshine and regular Friday 'waterings' at the Zelena Dolina restaurant. We would claim that they reached fruition thanks to the richness of the stories' sources, rather than fertilization with the bullshit that often accompanies military reminiscences.

The final judgment is yours!

Why a book? We asked ourselves the same question, especially after finding the wealth of humorous anecdotes available on various websites, notably ARRSE, the Army Rumour Service. The answer comes from the many that find themselves without Internet access, especially on operational tours, and from a suspicion that material committed to print might reach wider readership than an anecdote quickly relegated to page 4 or 5 of a blog or discussion thread. It also provides an opportunity to contribute to a worthwhile, related cause and Help for Heroes will receive £1 from the proceeds for every copy sold.

Thanks are due to the many contributors and sources that have given permission to include their stories here. Thanks, too, to all those characters that enacted these scenes in real life. Should you recognize yourself in any of the anecdotes, either starring or in a supporting role, then accept the appreciation of all those that smile, laugh or cry as they read.

Pull up a Sandbag is dedicated to all servicemen and women on active duty. If it raises a laugh in Afghanistan or Iraq it will have been a worthwhile endeavour. This dedication is also extended to include those who will see active duty, those who have seen active duty and those that still suffer its aftermath

Yes, it's Tommy this, an' Tommy that, an' spend less on defence,
But who walks the streets of Basra when the air is getting tense?
When the air is getting tense, boys, from Kabul to Kosovo
Who'll say goodbye to wife and kids, and shoulder pack and go?
Peter Pindar, *Sunday Telegraph December 2003*

Hasn't changed much, has it?

1. Jonathan Begins to Smile

"Once upon a time" seemed an appropriate way to open, but it didn't have the ring of truth. "Twice upon a time" would have been a step in the right direction, but I'd lost count of the number of false starts, so that was discarded too. It was only when I stopped raking through the problem of describing the beginnings that the dust settled, clarity returned and realisation dawned. History is defined more by those that record it than by fact. The solution was to just get on and write it ... so here goes!

It started as a night like a hundred others, or maybe a thousand, if I'm honest. Meeting with friends for a drink and a chat had become a well-worn habit that served to punctuate the end of the week, and the general pattern of the evening rarely changed. Greetings and news were exchanged fairly quickly before settling into the core activity of the evening, like brushing crumbs from the table-top to make way for the main course. Here the main course was a kind of conversational comfort food, chewing over topics we had revisited many times, recycling discussions but each time finding a new flavour to the argument or a twist that added zest to an otherwise bland subject.

It should come as no surprise that reminiscences were an unavoidable ingredient in the mix, given the membership of our select little group; ex-military, ex-Police, ex-Customs and Excise, plus a vague and disorganised individual who classified himself simply as 'ex'. We shared a slightly dark sense of humour, the cynicism common to those professions and a willingness to talk long, hard and late, provided that the accustomed conversational lubricants remained accessible. These could be brown, yellow or black, as long as they boasted alcoholic content and came in large glasses, though occasionally something small and golden did the trick. The vague and disorganised one preferred black, as it seemed a neutral colour and hence the closest he could get to making no choice at all.

On this particular evening, Bod had arrived first, as usual, but had ordered a complete round for the group. His confidence in the others' imminent arrival may have been based on strength of habit rather than attention to punctuality, but was justified as Plod and Sod[1] stamped into the bar before the last freshly-poured pint hit the counter. The vague and disorganised one arrived last, again as usual, and made the same excuse about the black stuff needing time to settle he had used a dozen times before. The others smiled indulgently, conscious of their own pet repetitions, and our gang of four settled into their customary seats at the corner table.

It wasn't long before we entered the relaxed part of the evening, replaying old conversations. These weren't the sterile, CD-like snippets exchanged at the bar, or the quick one-liner soundbites tossed across the room. Each anecdote was a carefully handled LP, played only by its owner, complete with the hiss and pops and crackles appropriate for its age. We sat back, listened and enjoyed, not noticing the occasional skips, as we knew each note and ornamentation from previous performances. The silences between were comfortable, as we each considered which stories to play next, but never long, due to calls of "Mine's a lager", "My round!" or Sod complaining "It's like a desert in here!"

Eventually, the vague and disorganised one provided an interlude by remarking on the weird and wonderful quirks of memory. He started by mentioning the clichéd distinction between a comic and a comedian (a comic says funny things, but a comedian says things funny). He continued, "I went to a comedy club last night and saw two excellent main acts. The first guy was a true comedian who told one funny story that lasted fifteen minutes. I could tell it to you now almost word for

---

[1] It's not unusual to find the confession "names have been changed, to protect the innocent". No confessions in this case; the names are those we used for each other, and none of us are, were, or will ever again be completely innocent.

word. The second had me laughing like a drain for twenty minutes with a non-stop barrage of well-timed one-liners, but I can't remember a single one. Doesn't the human mind work in wonderful ways!"

Plod chipped in with, "I heard a professional comedian tell that the only time his mind went completely blank was when a fan of his said, 'Go on then, be funny'. Two minutes later, someone mentioned his mother-in-law and twenty jokes immediately sprang to mind."

"I know what you mean," added Bod. "I can never tell the first story, but the moment one of you starts, it reminds me of one of my own. In fact, it's more of a cascade process than a simple knock-on effect; each one reminds me of three or four others. I guess it's the same for you because we start slowly, but there's never enough time to get them all in before closing time. Couldn't just be the effects of the beer, could it?"

Sod, nodding and looking extremely thoughtful, held our full and undivided attention as we waited for his pronouncement on memory. "Beers all round then?" he asked, and disappeared to the bar.

We'd hardly expected anything truly erudite at that stage of the evening, but it was unlike Sod to have nothing to say. He didn't disappoint. "Reminds me of the prisoner joke," he said on his return. We were hooked. "A prisoner was thrown into a dungeon and chained to the wall. As his eyes became accustomed to the gloom he could see a dozen others chained around the walls. Eventually the man next to him broke the silence, asking 'Know any jokes?' Every joke he told was greeted with howls of laughter from his fellow prisoners, until he finally exhausted his repertoire. After a short pause, one of the others said, 'fifty-three' and everyone laughed. The newcomer was puzzled when subsequent shouts of 'twenty-five', 'sixteen' and 'thirty-three' all had the room in stitches. His neighbour explained that every prisoner had told every joke they knew, and that these had been repeated until everyone knew all the jokes by heart. To save time telling the whole story, the jokes had been numbered. Each time someone mentioned a number, the prisoners remembered that joke and laughed. The newcomer thought he'd try this out but when he loudly proclaimed 'twenty-two!' it was followed by silence. Several numbers were called out by other prisoners during the next few minutes and all raised a laugh, so the newcomer tried again with 'thirty-one!' Again silence. Several shouts later, someone quietly mentioned 'twenty-two' and the room was filled with hysterical laughter.

'Just a minute!' complained the newcomer, 'I said twenty-two a while ago and nobody laughed.'

His neighbour turned apologetically towards him, 'Ah, it's the way you tell them!' he explained."

The link to memory was there, though not central to the story, but we could see the direction his thoughts had taken when he asked, "We're only prisoners of habit, but how many different stories do you think we've told each other in this room over the years?" None of us had a clue, and estimates varied wildly. "The only reliable way to find out would be to write them down," he continued. There was a brief clamour of voices as every one of us claimed to have had the idea to collect these stories in a written record, each claim pre-dating the previous by at least a year. The Monty Python team would have been proud of us. By this late stage of the evening the effects of our liquid intake were definitely in evidence, and it gradually became very important to write down as many of these tales, anecdotes and observations as we could remember. "For posterity!" declared Plod in the most earnest voice he could muster. "For posteriority!" countered Bod, "Same format, but perforate the pages."

Having all claimed the idea, a quick check around the table confirmed that we'd all made similar progress: none. This left us with an open choice for the post of scribe, uncluttered by questions of aptitude, experience or conventional logic. The only unanimous agreement was that the task should fall to just one of our company. Risk of duplication was an excellent excuse as we all back-pedalled to avoid putting any real effort into this "essential" work.

The question was resolved when three of the group realised that the vague and disorganised one, though not the best choice for the job, would offer least resistance of all to the nomination.[2] Bod, the most imaginative of the three, quickly came up with the rather arbitrary criterion of "name most suited to author of a work of humour". Thus, by process of elimination, the vague and disorganised one was saddled with the task.

That'll be me, then – Jonathan Smiles.

Here it is, finally; the product of a marriage of inebriate minds including, appropriately enough, something old, something new, something borrowed, something blue.

Seats at the corner table are all taken, so pull up a sandbag...

---

[2] Those of you who have waded through the purple prose will now know that four old farts got pissed, decided to write down some stories and at this point were about to decide who'd get lumbered with the task. Why it has taken five pages to say so is likely to remain a mystery. Don't be put off! The going gets easier from here on in.

2. Sprogs, Newbies, Wind-Ups and Wahs

We've all been there; finished our Basic Training and then begun military life at our first unit, running around camp from one location to the next in our desperate search for spirit level bubbles, tartan paint, keys for the indoor mortar range and the outdoor assault course, skirting board ladders, etc, etc. Sprogs and newbies provide easy targets, but squaddies show no mercy. Nor should they; how else will these innocents develop the resistance to survive a military career?

Mister Vice (of the Mess Variety)

There are many, many opportunities during a Service career to fall prey to practical jokes, with particular vulnerability when appearing as 'the new boy' in any situation. Sprogs are easy meat, but new arrivals to a unit who have previous tours under their belts are a harder target. By the time potential victims are promoted to Sergeant, most have developed the kind of awareness that makes them immune to practical jokes. There is a theory that claims this is the very reason Warrant Officers' and Sergeants' messes were invented. Learning the intricacies and traditions of Mess life and an additional, archaic uniform can be an expensive business, usually paid for in a currency of gin and tonic or bottles of port.

Those attending their first Mess dinner provide a target rich environment, but the most junior Sergeant inevitably becomes the main mark. He is appointed 'Mister Vice', a title that carries with it all sorts of additional duties; some seated in tradition, some in practice and necessity, but others down to nothing more than the sense of humour of the assembled company.

At a Squadron top table lunch, the newly promoted Mister Vice was briefed that after the main course the Squadron Sergeant Major (SSM) would bang his gavel to signify that he would like his biscuits to be served. The biscuits were then to be placed on a table to the side of the dining area, and Mister Vice was further briefed that on distribution of the said biscuits he should bow his head to the SSM and report "Sir, your biscuits are not broken, Sir." To lend credibility, it was explained that seventy-five years ago a fight had broken out amongst the Warrant Officers in a Guards mess over the lack of digestive biscuits and the War Office had decreed that biscuits were to be served by the youngest Sergeant in all messes from that day forward.

In due course, the gavel was banged to signify a comfort break and much to the merriment and amusement of all, the biscuits were delivered with much bowing and ceremony – as were five bottles of Port. On comes the light-bulb as Mister Vice thinks, "I am a cnut!

Saw Him Coming?

Young Sapper X was on his second day in the Unit after completing his Basic Training and Combat Engineer III Course a few days earlier. He was called over to the Troop G10 Store by one of the Troop Corporals, who informed him a section was tasked to clear an area of trees on the edge of the airfield. Two other Sappers and one of the Troop Lance Jacks were already clad in Husqvarna (chainsaw) PPE and busy checking that each chainsaw had its full inventory of spares prior to heading out on their tree cutting task. Sapper X was told to get the full PPE on ASAP. He proceeded to don his PPE (leather leggings/chaps, protective gloves, boot and shin guards and jacket) when the Troop phone rang, which Corporal T answered.

Corporal T wrote out a quick memo, placed it in a brown envelope and handed it to young Sapper X explaining that the memo had to be handed personally to the SSM, who was currently in his office. Sapper X was told to put on his helmet complete with visor and ear defenders; the section would be leaving their berets in the office to avoid getting them in crap state during the tree cutting, so he would need some kind of head dress at Squadron HQ.

Corporal T instructed Sapper X to make sure he was wearing his helmet correctly in the offices, including keeping the visor down and as he had signed for the chainsaw he would be using, to take it with him and to keep hold of it as it was a starred item. The section would get the rest of the kit loaded and meet him outside Squadron HQ in 10 minutes after he had hand-delivered the memo to the SSM.

"Make sure you wait for the Sergeant Major's reply before leaving his office," was Corporal T's final instruction.

Sapper X, not wanting to let anyone down in his first few days, eagerly rushed off with chainsaw in one hand, memo in the other, wearing full PPE, with helmet on and visor down! Our intrepid young Sapper entered Squadron HQ, marched up to the SSM's door and knocked. Hearing a bellowed "Enter!" he opened the door, marched up to the SSM's desk and halted smartly a foot from the desk, then handed the memo to the SSM, stating he had to wait for the reply.

Faced with a young Sapper in full PPE, helmet visor down and chainsaw in hand, the SSM calmly opened the envelope and read the following memo:

> *Sir,*
>
> *I completed my Basic Combat Engineer Course on Friday last week and was informed that I had to be at 33 Engineer Regiment (EOD) for first parade Monday morning. This completely messed my plans up as I was looking forward to a long weekend at the minimum after finally completing my Basic Training. I am pissed off to say the least, so I am kindly asking you to fill out a leave pass for me in order to give me a long weekend from this coming Friday. Fail to do so and I will start up this chainsaw and saw your fucking desk in half!*
>
> *Thank You,*
> *Sapper X*

Luckily, the SSM had a good sense of humour and even wrote a reply to Corporal X's Memo before sending the young Sapper on his way with no reprisals although no doubt he had a quiet word some time later with Corporal X (if SSM's words are ever quiet!).

A Box of Sparks

Whilst based in Paderborn, Sprogs were often sent to the stores for a 'box of sparks'! The usual thing was to send them back to confirm which colour was required.

Tube Trek

We had a Private Storeman who was sent to the QM Stores by MT section to get 'fallopian tubes' for some 4 Tonne vehicles. The QMS then sent him to the LAD for a 1043/5. The LAD sent him to the URS in the servicing bay, who told him it was a specialist item refurbished by the Medics. Off he wandered to the Med Centre where CMT medic type chap plainly asked "What size?"

Nearly a four-mile walk by the time he got back to his reception committee!

Direct Route

A young Gurkha undergoing driver training at Leaconfield had certainly already learned how to take orders. As he approached a roundabout the instructor said "Straight over" and the Gurkha did just that – went straight over the roundabout.

Report to Sergeant Fletcher

It was while I was at RAF Wattisham that an often used joke was carried out on newbies to the Phantom aircraft.

Most everybody has heard the one about sending a newbie for a left-handed screwdriver or for some elbow grease. This was a twist on that. Phantom aircraft carry external fuel tanks on the wings and they are called Sergeant Fletcher fuel tanks.

Well it's obvious, isn't it; we used to send them around the camp telling them to report to Sgt Fletcher. As most people were in on the joke they used to keep sending the poor sap onto someone else until that is they ended up at the fuel tank repair bay. It sometimes lasted for hours. Wasn't life fun!

The 25m Range Cleaning Kit

We lost count of the times in Northern Ireland where we got a new bloke to go to the CQMS stores for the 25m range cleaning kit. They would come back with 40m of rope and an old mattress. We would just sit back and watch as the idiot crawled the length of the pipe range, one end of the rope around his waist and the other tied to the mattress, then bite back the laughs as he struggled for twenty minutes trying to pull it through the range. Worked a treat every time!

The Temperature Indication Team

One of my personal favourites took place on board a Royal Navy Type 42 Destroyer. Just before a surface to air missile shoot, a list asking for volunteers for a very special duty was doing the rounds. It explained:

"As many of you are probably aware, a rocket propelled surface to air missile such as a Seadart can be a major hazard to marine plant life, especially if the rocket fuel has not combusted at the correct temperature. To that end it is important to assemble a Temperature Indication Team (TIT) in order to record the exact temperature of the flames coming out of the rocket motor on take-off. Obviously, there are some hazards with this task so all members of the TIT must be dressed correctly in full firefighting rig. Due to the blast of the rocket motor it is also mandatory to wear a safety harness to ensure no-one is blown over the side.

Once the team is assembled and briefed on their important task, they must then stand behind the missile launcher with a thermometer (to be signed out from sickbay prior to the launch). It is recommended that the thermometer be attached to a broom handle or similar, however this is at the discretion of the TIT leader. A few dry runs, under the watchful eyes of the rest of the ship's company, should be carried out so that the whole team is clear on their individual duties. Only once the team is fully conversant with the whole procedure and they are stood to behind the missile launcher can the firing take place."

I once saw a young Wren in tears because she hadn't been selected for the TIT. It was OK, though, because we promised she could be a line buoy lookout when we crossed the equator.

A Right Spanner

In 32 Armoured Engineer Regiment there used to be a crank spanner for the Centurions; jaws about six inches wide, head about a foot across, handle about three feet long and four inches wide. It weighed a ton. This item was kept in the guardroom, which was about a kilometre from the tank park at Monkey lager.

The usual wind-up was that a Cent AVRE would be turned over with the ignition off and the tank commander would tell the troop sprog that the engine needed turning over with the spanner. Off would go the sprog to the guardroom, eventually staggering back to the park with said spanner only to be greeted by the tank starting up just has he arrived back. Oh, the merriment as he realised he had to take spanner back to the guardroom!

Gibloons

Another favourite of mine used to be money-changing for Gibraltar. Money-changing forms would go out to all the messdecks about two days before getting into Gib and all the old hands would fill it in, letting the newbies put their names on it too. Needless to say, the newbies would be the only ones mustering at the ship's office for their 'Gibloons'.

Magnetic Water

The other classic was at RNAS Culdrose. One young green WAFU was sent to the stores for a bucket of magnetic water for the compasses in the Sea Kings. He was told that as it could affect the compasses in other helicopters, if he was overflown he had to lie over the top of the bucket.

Picture the scene: on the main perimeter road at RNAS Culdrose, which used to be busier than Heathrow for aircraft movements, one young WAFU, carrying a full-to-the-brim bucket (having been told not to spill any, as it was expensive). *Wocka, wocka*, a Sea King flies overhead. WAFU lies on top of bucket as it goes over, with one of the aircrew hanging out of door, taking piccies of this poor sod lying over the bucket.

He finally makes it back to squadron with a big wet circle on his shirt, to be met by all the lads mustered in the hangar and much mirth.

The Wah

Sometimes used to denote any wind-up or sprog-directed prank, the *wah* is more often the verbal response to a bone question asked by a superior (bone questions asked by juniors are dealt with very differently!). Also used within the British Army to signal an unnecessary response to an obvious or rhetorical question. The original question has often been posed by the wah-monger himself, as a set-up. Can become quite frustrating as you become paranoid about answering any question in case it is a wah!

As an example:

Steve: "Is that a can of beer in your hand Bill?"
Bill: "Yeah."
Steve: "Wah!"
Bill: "Bugger. Wah'd again!"

The Wah-Free Zone

A few years ago, on a Squadron range camp, we had some septics over on an exchange thing. The wahing got so bad that folk pretty much stopped talking to each other. A typical conversation might run:

"Alright Codename? How's things?" answered by,

"Is that a wah? Fuck off."

At the end of the week, come the Squadron smoker, the bar was deathly quiet with no-one speaking for fear of being wah'd. The seppos just thought we were strange (fair point really). It got so bad that the Badge had to make an announcement:

Badge: Right you fuckers, this is getting out of hand. From now on, the bar is a wah-free zone.

Seppo: What's a wah-free zone Sergeant Major?

Badge: Well, that's where you can't...

Entire Squadron: WAAAH!!!

Egg-Op Wahs

As a young cooky-boy I recall being sent to the Stores to get some tartan breadcrumbs for the scotch eggs... Bastards!

I felt better when one lad was told to 'put a fork in the bangers' before they were cooked for breakfast. He succeeded in using up all the forks in the mess hall.

The Chief Cook went ballistic.

Sandpaper Wah

I am currently in the middle of a rather amusing wah. I work at a gun factory with a lot of other ex-Forces types so the ancient art of wahing is not lost on many.

We have started charging a certain apprentice for the amount of sandpaper he uses. It has been going on for nearly three months now and the poor lad is so broke he is making every sheet last as long as possible. A couple of the lads have managed to get him to flash by nicking his sandpaper. He was almost in tears last week when he complained, "Seriously guys it's not fair.

I can't afford to pay for all of you to use my sandpaper. I am only on an apprentice's wage."

He has even started writing his name on the back of his sandpaper and is threatening to put in a formal complaint the next time he catches someone stealing his sandpaper.

There are no signs of any realisation dawning on him, after all this time, and I'm not sure he'd recognize the wah if we spelled it out. If a sequel to 'Sandbag' comes out next year, there's every chance I'll be providing an update and a claim to the longest running wah in living memory!

The Bunk Light Bill

This has just reminded me of another good naval one. Newbie joins the ship, settles in and after his first week is told about the bill for his bunk light. Said newbie then spends the rest of the month either reading by torchlight or just getting into his scratcher and going to sleep. End of the month, there he is standing at the regimental office trying to pay his bill!

Beer Tokens

As a young Sapper just out of training, upon arrival at my new unit in BAOR one of the older lads asked me if I had my beer tokens for the weekend. "Beer tokens?" says I.

"Yep, beer tokens" says he. "You go to the pay office and ask to buy beer tokens. You pay Deutschmarks and collect these tokens that get you cheaper beer down town. Paying with tokens brings the cost down to Squadron Bar prices."

So off I run to the pay office with a handful of Deutschmarks, to get my beer tokens.

The pay clerk was actually quite polite as he explained the situation to me. He didn't laugh at all ... until I walked away.

Target Laser Sight

The trick NIG (Billy, newboy) gunners in our lot used to fall for was the old 'TLS routine' (Target Laser Sight, for you non Chieftain wallopers out there).

The Troop Commander would shout:

"Young'n, grab that TLS and take it across the QM(T)s for an exchange, like kidder."

As said TLS is passed over to him, the Troop Cpl would generally add, whilst backing rapidly away, "Son, see the radiation hazard sign? Means you gotta suit up, like, in case you drop it on the way and it leaks." (In fact, the TLS only contained tritium or trilux [like a watch] if memory serves.)

Not five minutes later, said trooper is marching across the tank park in full Noddy order, over-boots, S10 and gloves, the lot, with a boxed-up TLS in outstretched arms. By the time he gets to the Tech store, they are all in on it, suited and booted too, and everyone he passes there and back again runs a mile in terror when they see him coming.

Back to hanger and he is asked (from 100 yards across the park) to blot, bang, rub everything he touches before he hands it back to the fitter waiting in the turret.

Said CFN then pops head out of turret 'sans NBC gear' and shouts at terrified NIG.

"WAH!"

3. If It Ain't Raining, It Ain't Training!

More sweat, less blood. Train hard, fight easy. Worldwide there are scores of expressions of this sentiment. It's just as well most of us accept the reasoning behind this, as many training activities include an embuggerance factor that can be soul destroying. Then there's the weather. Perhaps it's divine discouragement from warlike activities, but why does it always seem to rain on training? It's possible for negative impressions to overshadow the positive benefits, but one redeeming feature about training is the number of incidents that range from amusing to hilarious.

Camouflage & Concealment

Picture the scene: the Army Ranger Wing (ARW), Irish Special Forces, is down in the Glen of Imaal on a sniper selection course. Trainees are given five minutes to leg it and hide in the surrounding countryside while the Rangers look the other way. The Rangers then try to find them using binoculars, with hunters on the ground they can move around via radio.

Meanwhile, a platoon of reservist recruits is also on the area, getting their first lesson on camouflage and concealment. The corporal taking the lesson has them form a semi circle, about twenty feet away from him. He starts into his lesson, going through how to apply cam cream and all that, when one of the hunters starts walking towards them.

The corporal inquires what the problem is but the hunter raises an index finger in a 'shut-the-fuck-up' gesture, while his radio crackles away and a message comes through.

"Move left two metres."

The hunter is now in the middle of the semicircle, between the recruits and the corporal, when he gets *"at your feet"* on the radio. Next thing, everyone hears a voice say, "Ah bollocks! Am I binned?" as a sniper, who was a clump of grass a few seconds ago, rises to his feet, bang in the centre of the unsuspecting but now amazed and impressed reservists!

The hunter replies, "No, mate, you'll get another go. Good effort, though. Now fuck off back to the transport."

The Corporal Instructor and reservists are all gobsmacked, absolutely speechless, until the corporal says, "And by the end of this lesson I expect you all to do *better* than that!"

Taking Precautions

I remember an overnight stop in Nuremburg during a summer camp trip to Kochel am See in Bavaria. Enquiring at the local USMC base as to where to go for the night, one of our brothers from 'across the pond' informed us there was a local ladies' establishment called 'The Wall' just down the road, so off we trotted like good little explorers, to find out what this 'Wall' offered. Lo and behold (!) it turned out to be an 'establishment of ill-repute'. Not blessed with an overabundance of beer tokens, we drew lots to decide who would be the lucky Squaddie to lighten the load. To protect the not-so-innocent, let's just refer to the lucky stout feller as Signalman V. So off goes Signalman V into the place and does the dirty deed...

Later that night, when the Troop Commander finds out his boys have been frequenting such an establishment, he isn't too happy. All stood in front of him, he asks Signalman V if he 'took any precautions' whilst in the brothel, to which the siggie replies: "Aye, I did Boss. I gave Signalman C my wallet."

The Exploding Field Kitchen

Our unit was on exercise in Germany during the late 80s, deep in one of the Fatherland's densest, darkest, spookiest forests. We were all in the usual harbour area setup, most of us in perimeter defensive positions for Stand To prior to breakfast, when an almighty explosion went off in the HQ area. Fearing the worst, we all stampeded towards the source of the explosion, to help or give first aid to the injured, only to be confronted by a dazed but otherwise uninjured 'Hot Plate Specialist' wandering around what used to be the Cook's Tent, covered head-to-toe in the full morning menu of beans, eggs, sausages, bacon and other breakfast delights.

Apparently, the fire extinguisher in that little compartment in the middle of the Number 5 Cooker (impressed with the technical terminology?) had overheated and exploded (after this, and maybe other similar incidents, all Number 5s ended up with a bar welded across 'that little compartment').

Who said life as an Egg Operator in the Army is without its risks? Then again, ears still ringing from the explosion, they may well have said 'whisks'!

What Point Water Point?

Despite being on the same side, there always appears to be a slight (!) antipathy between units/sub-units and their superior headquarters. This was never more evident than during my first posting in the late 70s and early 80s.

When 16 Parachute Brigade was disbanded, 9 Independent Parachute Squadron RE lost the 'Independent' from its title and became part of 36 Engineer Regiment. The Regiment was based in Maidstone, but 9 Squadron remained in Aldershot and retained its Para role. The chain of command seemed tense, rather than taut!

Every opportunity was taken for digs at the 'opposition', usually good-natured but sometimes carrying a harder edge. Against this background, the Squadron 2IC should have expected repercussions when he complained during an FTX that the Squadron was not busy enough, being used to the higher tempo of Airborne operations. The reply came as a series of additional, short-notice tasking orders that ensured no rest until ENDEX.

My Troop's immediate challenge was to construct a brigade water point, with a very tight timeline for delivery.

Recce completed, stores ordered and site preparation under way, I took the time to reflect whether this was one of the planned FTX tasks or a spurious addition by RHQ to keep us busy. The former meant we could expect 'customers' (units expecting potable water from the tasked delivery time onwards) but if it was just an RHQ-inspired task, then the water was unlikely to be used. Ever mindful of environmental issues, and aware that the River Avon was close downhill from the water point, I mentioned my concerns to SHQ and they relayed to RHQ, querying whether we should treat the water or not (sedimentation and filtration would prove that we'd accomplished the task, but full treatment would result in tens of thousands of litres of water containing more chlorine than the countryside deserved).

The RHQ reply was immediate and disdainful: "The order called for potable water. Just get on with it."

Deadline met and reported, it became plain that the task had originated with RHQ when they immediately ordered that the water point be dismantled. The reply was nowhere near as quick when we asked what they would like us to do with 30,000 litres of chlorinated water.

The resulting yellow fan on Salisbury Plain was still visible over two months later as we flew in for a drop at Eversleigh DZ. Looking down from the C130, I couldn't help thinking about childhood winter games involving handwriting and yellow snow. Pity it hadn't occurred to me at the time!

Compo Consequences

I can remember taking home a couple of 24-hour packs to show my old man what we lived on in the field and he helped himself over two days – breakfast, dinner and tea. He even had the balls to say I was spoilt on exercise with this type of delicious food!

He then went five days without a shite and had to buy prune juice to get his bowels to function correctly again!

Oh how I laughed!

You Had to Laugh!

The fundamental skill that all squaddies should possess is the ability to laugh at absolutely anything. I remember standing on parade at Wathgill Camp, North Yorkshire in a blizzard. We'd fucked up on the ranges so they just left us out there whilst drifts were building up at our feet. I'd never been that miserable before. The Geordie lad on my left had his ear full of compacted snowflakes like an icy hearing aid. He turned to me, a big snot string hanging from his nose, and said:

"Howay man, this is nee fuckin' laffin' matta."

He said it with such a deadpan expression that I and six blokes within earshot all cracked up completely!

Not Only Bears...

In a previous life I had the honour of teaching young crows how to be grown up, including how to wash, eat and shit in the field. The highlight of my lesson was a trick I'd learnt from the old and bold that taught me (probably QM 2 Para now). I'd explain that it was tactically, as well as environmentally important that combat turds should be properly buried and/or camouflaged. I then expressed my indignation at how the local FTA was covered in poorly laid bumsnakes and how one could 'hardly turn over a stone without finding one around here'. At that, I would turn over the nearest stone to reveal a Mister Hanky winking at me with compo bog roll covered in skids.

"This really grips my shit!" I'd proclaim, before stuffing a handful of tissues into my mouth, ensuring I smeared some of the muck around my lips.

Of course, the 'shit' was really a mashed up choccy bar and the tissues were covered in chocolate sauce, but the look on the young crows' faces was priceless.

You could see them mentally composing letters to their mums asking to be allowed back home![3]

---

[3] In my day, we'd have told the next intake to ensure that the chocolate was substituted with the real thing. Now *that* would be a funny story! [Editor]

The Acorn Club

Years ago, when your chap would stick out like an 'arm holding a blood orange', your stomach muscles hadn't given out and you weren't a fat bastard, you could still be a proud member of the Acorn Club. I remember quite fondly those days with 33 Engineer Regiment EOD...

Many will remember the joys of the decontamination line after completing an NBC task (usually leak-sealing and packaging an item of unexploded or leaking ordnance containing a chemical agent). We were dressed in Gucci yellow rubberized suits which zipped up dry-suit style from behind, across the shoulders, making it impossible for the wearer to unzip on their own. Inside this outer shell we carried full Self Contained Breathing Apparatus (SCBA) and we were harry blacked into an inner fuel suit, which itself was worn over other layers of protective clothing. Movement wasn't easy!

Usable duration of the SCBA tanks varied, depending on levels of physical activity and the fitness of the user, and a whistle sounded to warn that the tanks were nearing depletion. This usually signalled ten minutes left out of a fifty-minute set, but if you were a fat barsteward, or not very fit you might get just twenty-five minutes of normal time, with only five minutes left when your whistle started! IT PAYS TO BE FIT!!! It certainly didn't pay to be still sealed in when the whistling stopped, as the blue colour when you were eventually unwrapped would no doubt scare the medics.

The slow trudge back to the decontamination line was often completed with the warning whistle sounding. It must have resembled something out of an S&M Tellytubbies episode. Any civvy looking in from a distance would have been forgiven for thinking they were being invaded by life-sized orange and yellow rubber sex toy aliens communicating by whistling to each other.

You were in your own world in one of those suits. On one particular day I remember being about fourth in line, idly thinking things like 'I hope that fucking whistle doesn't stop' and 'Why is that bastard in front of me when his whistle isn't even going?" when, suddenly, more unexpected thoughts popped up: "Why is that idiot waving at me?" followed by "Why is he on the floor thrashing around?" and then "Oh fuck! He needs unzipping!"

In this case, the idiot was an unnamed Sergeant who I actually liked and I apologise now for any brain damage caused due to me thinking it was funny and thus extending his oxygen-free period in his vacuum pack.

No medals for that heroic action, but now I am at the back of the fucking queue! Returning to my own little world, the thoughts are not so idle after the recent demonstration and my mind is working overtime. "Hey mate, I hope you don't stop whistling. We'll be in a big pile of poo if you do ... Oh my God, I'm talking to a whistle!"

Anyway, after making real good friends with my whistle I am finally at the decontamination line. After a quick wash and a couple of jabs to the groin by the really funny blokes with nasty big brushes, I am ready for the next layer. After a few more disrobing sessions, completed with whistle-time to spare, I find myself bollock naked with the freezing cold mid-November air hitting my body, and I'm ready for the final hose-down.

After surveying the situation my heart sank. The onlookers included some women and the bloke in front of me, LCpl Hugh Mungus, was slowly strutting to the shower, hands on hips, showing off something that really should have been attached to a horse and not a human being. He even had the confidence to shout out, "Hey girls remember it's cold!" I looked down into my cupped hands. Oh fuck! Already my chap was retreating like a tortoise's head into its shell, and I hadn't even got in the shower yet. A deep breath, a big sponge in one hand and soap in the other, and off I went...

"Why has that woman got no tits?" I heard someone shout.

"Tense Vic, tense!" I told myself, as I checked out who the joker on the water pump was. Corporal Schwartz wore a sadistic smile as "AAAAAAAAARGH!" four hundred million bars of *fucking freezing* cold water did its best to rip my skin off. "Bastard!" I shouted, and then, thinking defiance was the best option, I stuck my arse out of the side of the shower and shouted "Look into my Jap's eye!" That was not the smartest move, as the four hundred million bars of pressure immediately doubled.

Finally it was over. I looked down to make sure my skin was still attached and was pleased to find out that my chap had not been blasted off. It had just disappeared. A few more jokes about women's bits and the pain began to fade. I was warming up in a nearby tent, wondering how I could get my own back on Cpl Schwartz, when he entered the recovery tent and handed me a newly laminated business card. It had a picture of two tiny acorns with an even smaller twig still attached, complete with my name and membership number.

I had been officially awarded Acorn Club honours and was accepted into this small, but certainly not elite EOD Club. Sixteen years later, I still have my Acorn Club membership card. Every time I look at it, my willy shrinks and I have flashbacks to many freezing times on the decontamination line. Am I really convinced when I tell myself they were happy days?

Redskin Encounter

This story came my way by passage of the Squadron Bar, in this case the RE Squadron Bar (with which, as an ex 'Wedgey', I am most familiar). Now before embarking on my story, I don't think it would be right for me to plough on without providing a little expansion and illumination as to what exactly Squadron Bars are and why they provide the setting for so many tales of soldierly 'misadventure'.

There are many different squadron bars, be they beneath 'ataps' in Belize, in sand-bagged bunkers in Bosnia or – the most prolific and infamous of all – atop the three-storey, barrack buildings of Cold War Germany. Regardless of the setting or size, they all have a common thread running through them; they are a bar for the Squadron, run by a member of the Squadron, without the need to make profit, for the express purpose of getting absolutely fucking wankered whenever said Squadron should request.

Maybe it's to further that end, but the mythical and often philosophical Barman is usually selected not for his snow-white disciplinary record, nor for book-keeping prowess, but for his tendency towards alcoholism, mixed with a general disposition of indifference regarding his career. His selection, wherever possible and usually preferable, is often seen as 'a stepping-stone to Civvy Street'.[4]

In Germany the Squadron Bar concept was – as one of my Section Commanders once said, whilst sitting in a pool of his own piss and covered in suspicious brown freckles – 'a beautiful thing'. Located atop a three-story building housing some 150 soldiers between the ages of 18 and 35, the Squadron Bar made up the attic space and was ground only for members of the squadron or the bravest of guests. The barrack blocks looked like those from WWII movies (and in fact were!) that housed garrisons of German troops, often seen grabbing their helmets and weapons and scrambling out over cobbled pathways in the dark of night (klaxons blaring in the background) only to get gunned down by cigar-smoking American troops firing Tommy guns from the hip, and lobbing pineapple-shaped grenades (for those of you who have seen the *Dirty Dozen*).

Women were hardly ever seen except on special occasions as guests of the OC or some other 'grown-up.'

They were strange places, lit often like the bunker scene in Oliver Stone's *Platoon*, but without the dope. Anything went: involuntary defecation at the bar, or passing mulched-up pea-nuts mixed with vomit from mouth to mouth, or all-over body-

---

[4] In BAOR it was considered perfect 'preparation' for a soldier soon to become a civilian to take over the Squadron Bar, freeing him from much of the military tedium and giving him a suitable period to re-immerse and transition seamlessly into civilian life – and if he could manage to earn himself a few quid by 'fiddling the books' then it was considered he would fare even better! Civilian employers of the period must have wondered what the fuck the Army was doing to people – everyone that left was an overweight piss-head with a major attitude problem. Then again, they probably would have fitted right in.

hair shaving. It was, at its best, a freak show. Truly an awesome place that deserves a book all of its own ... but that's for another time.

Now, back to the reason I actually sat down tonight, the matter of the Squaddie and the Squaw...

The Squadron Bar where I met Tom was in Vitez, central Bosnia. In most cases, 1995 life for Sappers in Vitez was a little quiet, normality was setting in and the resident field squadron, to which I was not part, was taking some time out to fix up the bar. The Squadron Bar in this case was a collection of containers that were fastened together and surrounded by sandbags. I don't remember a great deal else about it other than on a certain night there would be a special guest appearance of 'Mystic Smeg', who would provide hilarious predictions about what would happen first to Bosnia in the coming week and then the field squadron, especially their management personnel.

I had been in many times before, but on the night in question my eye was drawn to a strange, human-sized, 'johnny-clad-cock' figure in the corner of the bar. I'd like to say I recognized Tom, but that would be inaccurate. Naked, he was wrapped as tightly as his mates could manage, mummy-like, from head to toe, in cling film. It was a weird sight, and it wasn't until they cut his head free that I recognized my old 'Junior Bleeder' colleague. It was then that the usual haven't-seen-each-other-in-eight-years conversation kicked in. He was still completely wrapped, apart from his head, but he had been lifted and propped in the corner of the bar to prevent him toppling over.

Me: Where you been then, mucker?
Tom: Oh, you know, here and there. You?
Me: Same. Here and there. Fancy a beer?
Tom: Yeah, go on then.
Me: Nice costume by the way. Suits you.
Tom: Thanks.
Me. Not serious mate, you look like a right twat.

Anyway, after Tom had 'swamped' himself ('swamping' is the Army euphemism for pissing oneself) a few times and threatened to shit in his 'wrap', it was commonly agreed that he should be released and allowed to don some normal clothing. We shot the shit some more and then a friend pressed him to tell the story of the 'Squaw in Medicine Hat'.

Tom looked away and ordered more beer. Even pushed a second and third time, he continued to evade. It was evident from his deep discomfort that something dark, something horrible, something unspeakable even, had happened in that strange town in Canada. It wasn't until much later that we finally broke through Tom's psychological defence systems and got him to spill the beans...

"It had been a night like any other," he said, "pissing it up at Medicine Hat after another hard day on the range. I normally never trap, so I was surprised when this Indian squaw started giving me the eye. Several beers later, she was looking almost female and I thought, 'if I keep going like this, I might just be able to stomach fucking her'. I thought I was in."

He explained that the main problem was likely to be the smell, which was – or so he had heard, being himself a Squaw virgin – fucking disgusting. As the night went on, he had calmed himself by repeating, 'don't go down on her, don't go down on her. It'll be OK, no need to worry.' Beer was consumed, ash-trays filled and emptied, and by the time he left, Tom – now totally 'shee-eye-ters' – had forgotten all his woes about the Squaw's box and its stench and was fondling her rampantly. They removed to her place of abode.

The story resumed with them both in bed and the squaw giving Tom a blow job. He continued:

"I was worried that she would move her nether regions upwards towards my face, but she seemed content to give me a blow job without need of reciprocal action. All progressed well. Then without warning, she pivoted round (I almost shouted 'No!') and seated herself firmly upon my face. I stopped breathing and hoped she would get off, but her wriggles told me otherwise. By this time I was in urgent need of a breath and tried bobbing my head to find a potential source of uncontaminated air to breathe in. She took this as moves to evade giving her the pleasure she obviously thought she was entitled to and seated down firmer still.

Suffocated beneath the foul smelling orifices, I craned my neck back and took the breath I had most feared. I almost puked. (fucking minger!) A rotten fish and bum-gravy cocktail filled my nostrils. I couldn't get away. I considered punching her or sticking a finger in her arse to get her to move, but she wasn't moving. I now remembered, with a sense of complete futility, that she was as fat as a carnival float and I just sort of ... gave up. A calm descended over me and so I stuck my tongue back in for a second try. It was gopping, but I thought I could manage, so I went for it, doing my best porn-star impression.

It was then that I felt her stiffen, and the muscles in her lower back and buttocks become taught. She stopped gobbling and seemed to tense. 'Oh yes,' I thought, 'she's getting off!'. I smiled with joy...

She then let out a thunderous fart. A fart so powerful I actually felt it across my face and hair. It stank. I retched but managed not to throw up. I threw her off but she seemed not to care and jumped back on top of me. As long as the orifices from hell were away from my face, I would persevere. I had come this far after all; I had to see it through. I lay perfectly still as she jumped on me, holding my breath long enough for the fart smell to dissipate."

By this time everyone in the Squadron Bar was staring in a state of utter disgust at Tom. But he went on...

"Some time later I collapsed and fell asleep. I woke up in the morning, thankfully without the immediate memories of the horrible night before. I went for a piss. I stared at the toilet bowl, laughing to myself at memories of the nightclub and the general gopping-ness of the Squaw in bed in the next room. What was I fucking thinking of, shagging something like that? I checked my manhood for strange objects and growths and was thankful that everything looked normal. I turned on the tap and washed my hands, glancing up at the shaving mirror above the basin.

It was then I saw it. A huge piece of tomato skin stuck to my fucking forehead! With that, I remembered the horrific events of the night before. Aaaaargh! I went into a kind of involuntary spasm dance as I danced around the bathroom trying, without touching, to get the indigestible piece of Squaw food from my forehead by flicking water at it (it had kind-of hardened itself on there). I'd heard that tomato skin is not digested by the human body, but did not know it could be fired from the arse on the blast of a fart with such force it would literally glue itself to a human forehead."

Everyone at the Bar was in tears of laughter, but it was clear to see that although he joked about it now, the events had a deep and lasting effect on Tom.

"I haven't been down on anyone since, and that was three years ago," he admitted. "I'm fucking serious! You should go through something like that and then try staring eye-to-eye at some gopper's starfish, you fuckin' knobbers!"

We laughed even harder and Tom ordered another beer.

Egg Banjo – Food of the Gods!

As soldiers will tell, one of the best treats is an 'egg banjo'. The reason for the word 'banjo' is very easy to recognise when you eat the said banjo for the first time. It is said an Army marches and fights on its stomach; the British Army marches and fights fuelled by its glorious egg banjos!

The banjo is a very emotive subject and must be considered at great length. Many an SQMS will have been saved by his egg/bread combo supply, and many a gunner/loader spared a thick ear on the quality and frequency of banjos produced. Grown and experienced soldiers have been reduced to tears at the lack/poor quality or taste of the banjo.

My preferred method, and a popular favourite, is as follows. The banjo must be cooked in a dixie lid, over a petrol cooker that should sound like the afterburner of a jet fighter. The fat/lard/oil/OM18/75/13 must be almost smoking, with perhaps a few pine needles, chinagraph lead, twigs, cotton waste, a black substance that builds up over some time (still no idea what it is) or burnt compo sausage bits still clinging to the pan. The egg should then be cracked into the dixie. The fat being very hot will ensure that the edge of the egg white will become crispy and brown. A honey colour is preferred, with the underside the same consistency and colour. The sunny side up must be runny and the base of the yoke hard.

This allows two methods of eating to take place.

Firstly, you can break your egg and mix in your favoured sauce, HP/Daddies brown or Heinz/HP tomato or dare I say both! This, sadly, will reduce the likelihood of a true banjo scenario, particularly for the new troop leader. An unbroken yoke will still allow the eating method of 'bite and suck' preferred by old sweats and trained banjo eaters. The sauce mix may still be applied.

Method two involves breaking the egg whilst frying. This will prevent many of the previous mishaps and is good for 'O' Groups as it prevents the embarrassment of dripping egg onto the OC's map. Awareness of this method may prevent a thick ear for an unskilled provider, who can always use the 'I thought you were off to an O Group' excuse. A flipped egg may also be needed to prevent jealous repercussions, as a small amount of runny egg on the chin is a definite tell-tale sign of contentment. Salt sprinkled over, whilst the banjo is still hot and un-sauced, is a personal thing.

Finally, the bread; preferably on the wrong side of fresh. Not mouldy, but a little 'gone'. Old RAOC bread was very good and was just the right shape (slightly round) and was labelled with the day of production. This was always appreciated as it reminded you how many days you had missed whilst in the OP/CV/barn/bunker/site guard or Ops Room.

However, new methods of bread production still allow for the spread of the 'not too fresh egg', which tend to flatten on cracking. A handprint of undetermined origin must also appear on the outer side of each bread slice.

The time of the day for a banjo bears no relation to its ability to lift morale. A wave of the hand containing a banjo (tea mug in the other), whilst sat on top of a tank/recce vehicle, to a passing infanteer carrying large quantities of equipment is a massive morale boost to anyone. Stepping down into your basher, whilst piss wet through, and being handed a banjo is like Christmas to a Squaddie! Walking towards the Sqn/Regt leaguer post shovel recce, O Group or maintenance period when a few dozen cookers are producing that slightly burnt, sweet and smoky aroma is almost majestic. Nothing brings a soldier to order quicker than the shout of "Banjos anyone?"

Remember that eggs were rationed during World War II. How on earth the British Army fought so well and maintained its morale through those dark, banjo-rationed times we in the modern Army will never know!

4. Barracks, Boredom, Bulling Boots and Bullshit

Having equipped a bunch of squaddies with the optimum combination of skills, fitness, teamwork and inspiration for their operational role, we have also reduced their resistance to the tedium of life in barracks. Nothing is more prone to mischief than a squaddie with energy, initiative and nothing to spend it on.

An Unwelcome Wedding Guest

At a highland wedding given by 'professional Scots' all of we groomsmen were dressed by Geoffrey's of Glasgow in a particularly psychedelic tartan – including a certain Englishman of the Gazelle-driving variety. Annoyed at having to dress up as a porridge wog, RH cut a hole at cock height in his rented kilt, with a matching hole in the back of the sporran – an expensive badger hair one! He then spent the remainder of an otherwise very posh wedding guzzling malt and asking various female guests to guess what was in his sporran – with a variety of good-humoured, albeit slightly shocked, responses until, that is, he asked the bride's mother – a very dour and bitter/twisted lady from darkest Inverness.

Eventually he was ejected from the wedding. I believe the groom was asked by the bride's family to investigate the cost of professionally removing him from the wedding pics... and I know he had to pay about £300 for the damage to his rented Rob Roy costume.

Grandfather's Medals

Remembrance Day and the Squadron is in No. 2 Dress, lined up for inspection before marching to the church. The OC and SSM are working their way down the line. Having inspected half the squadron, all assembled hear the SSM suddenly explode into an apoplectic fit.

"What the fuck do you call that? Who the hell told you that you could wear that piece of shite?"

"It was my granddad's, Sir," came the reply, "so I thought I should wear it, it being Remembrance Day."

"Not when your granddad was in the effin Waffen effin SS you shouldn't and especially not when it's an Iron Cross!"

Christmas Cheer

I remember getting jiffed with another bloke to deliver Christmas cards to all the married quarters from the Squadron one year...

When we were nearly finished, we got to the house of one of the unit headbangers. Using our powers of deduction we realised something was amiss. The contents of the house were getting chucked out of the windows into the garden. Primal roars were coming from the bedroom while the TV and the stereo came sailing out onto the grass.

The bloke's wife and two kids were stood at the front gate. The kids were crying and the Missus occasionally shouting back at the house "You mad bastard! Why don't you fuck off and leave us?" This would cause an escalation in the noise and another item of furniture would escape into the garden.

What did we do? We watched for five minutes then my mate wandered up to the wife, who by now was sobbing uncontrollably as her life fell apart. He stuck the card in her mitt, and winked at her.

"Merry Christmas from the Squadron, love!"

As we made to leave, the loon stuck his head out the bathroom window and shouted, "Hey fellas, what time does the Christmas do start?"

Class!

Stamp of Disapproval

With the possible exception of the victim, we all enjoy a prank. Some of the most elaborate japes can be a damp squib, however something seen as just a bit of a giggle can explode into a truly great practical joke.

A while ago I was covering a stores job for a mate while he was on leave. Whilst killing time, waiting to get knocked off on a Friday afternoon, I decided to change the words on his stamp (appointment, unit details, changeable date in the middle – you know the type) to read "I am a lazy fat cnut". Not rocket science, you will agree but by the Monday I had completely forgotten that I had done it. My only intention was for him to stamp something, swear, and then have to spend ten minutes putting his job title back together.

Nearly a month later, he was fucking livid with me and I really thought he was going to kick off. He hadn't noticed for a whole month, and had sent stuff to the CO, RSM, QM, and to other units all over the world.

He started to get the feedback about a week later, with some people sending memos to 'Cpl Bunting, the lazy fat cnut'. Even with all these clues, there was plenty of 'flash', but no 'bang'.

He only found out when submitting his end of month accounts. The RQMS pointed it out to him, and also informed him he would have to re-do the month's paperwork, track down stuff he had already sent to people and start apologising.

I got a bit of a rifting from the boss myself, for being the perpetrator, but was let off any action being taken as the silly sod should have noticed (besides, I think the boss saw the funny side as he was giggling while trying to bollock me!). My mate eventually accepted this, along with the consolatory beer I bought him, and he saw the funny side in the end.

Without intending it, minimum effort produced maximum results. I wish I'd had a bit of foresight and had changed the words into something a bit less playground, but there you go.

So, if you work with someone who uses one of those stamps, get a spare letter set from the stationery store and, when their back is turned, do it. They may notice straight away, or you might strike comedy gold!

Chilli Con Carnage

One Saturday on camp at Carver Barracks a fellow 'orphan' Cpl Smith and myself had come to the conclusion that after several beers for breakfast, it was safe to say that no brain cells were working, and the only thing to do was rig Corporal S's kettle with a little surprise, then get someone to make us a cup of tea.

A few wires, batteries, some harry black masking tape, and an outdoor sound unit later and we were ready. Just a few more drinks were needed before we went out to lure some unsuspecting person back for tea (all you perverts out there, stop thinking what you're thinking). Anyway, back to drinking. It was truly amazing how much beer the average 'orphan' could stash in their room in preparation for weekends and never get caught during inspections. Anyway, off we went to find someone, giggling like a couple of schoolgirls. An hour or two later, after failing miserably in our mission to find an unsuspecting fellow 'orphan', we cancelled the mission and decided it was time to cook lunch on the one burner that worked in the small kitchen thing in the accommodation block. (And yes, quaff some more beer!).

Big pan on stove; in went bacon, sausages and chopped chicken. As we proceeded to drink more beers and the food started to crisp on the outside Corporal Smith decided we needed to spice up our 'all-in', so he disappeared and quickly came back with a chilli pepper looking thing, which he then carefully laid in the pan. Suddenly a cloud of smoke appeared out of the pan. Corporal Smith, thinking this would be a good time to savour the great fragrance of our cooking, stuck his head into the smoke and inhaled deeply. Instantly he was on his knees coughing and spluttering, his eyes were bloodshot, and I am sorry to say all I could do was laugh.

Why would anyone stick their head in a load of smoke and keep their eyes open? I was laughing so much I didn't realise that the whole room was almost full of this acrid chilli smoke. As soon as I started to feel my eyes burning I legged it out of the room with Corporal Smith in hot pursuit.

We stood outside the door for a moment in agony and trying to breathe in some fresh air when it dawned on us... stove is on, pan still on stove, smoke coming under the door. In an unbelievably selfless act of bravery Corporal Smith said, "Vic get your arse in there and turn it off, there's a brave chap" (or words to that effect!). I opened the door and peeked in... My lungs went on fire and "Fuck you!" was all I could get out. Corporal Smith swiftly turned and sprinted back to his room. I was still laughing as I made attempts to blow the smoke back under the door. Seconds later he arrived back with S10 respirator on and shouted "Gas! Gas! Gas!" before disappearing into the cloud of smoke. I kid you not, 'Red Hot Chilli Peppers' burnt on an equally red hot frying pan give off a vapour that is ten times more powerful than CS pellets!

Seconds later Sapper Spiker arrived and helped me up from the floor "What's up?" came the innocent question. No good, I was laughing so hard I could hardly speak. To top it off Corporal Smith appeared out of the kitchen with S10 still on, absolutely howling with laughter. Poor Sapper Spiker must have had an uncharacteristic mature moment, as he just asked if we wanted to go for a beer.

So much for the chilli, but there you are thinking I have forgotten about the kettle. Well you would be both right and wrong. Right now I have not forgotten about the kettle. Back then we had completely forgotten about the kettle.

It was agreed that we order a Chinese take-away from nearby Saffron Walden before heading out to Cambridge for a night on the taps. An hour later in Corporal Smith's room, the three of us were sat on his bed and stuffing ourselves with Chinky chicken curry and bags of spring rolls when Sapper Spiker decided he wanted a cup of tea.

Now, at this point you would think that the two pranksters who had rigged the kettle hours before would remember this and make their excuses to leave the room for a moment. Wrong again. In fact, we were sitting at the end of the bed with the kettle on a table at head height and about two feet away when Sapper Spiker leaned between us and grabbed the kettle.

BAAAANG! Suddenly there was Chinese flying everywhere and I couldn't hear anything but a loud ringing in my ears. Through the smoke-filled, take-away-splattered room I could see Sapper Spiker on his knees with his hands over both ears, moaning in agony. Corporal Smith was laughing and pointing at where the kettle used to be. We quickly opened every window we could find in the block to let the smoke escape. It was lucky we did, as we found out later on the guard shift had been searching the entire camp looking for the seat of explosion of the suspected IED that had been heard on camp!

You will be pleased to know that the kettle was still working and made many a good brew after that day.

The Cresta Run

(A Navy Tale with thanks to Tony Groom, author of 'Diver')

We were once at DEODS (Defence Explosive Ordnance Disposal School) doing a mine radiography course (yes, you can X-ray a mine to see what's inside it. You may want to see how it works, and how it is triggered). We were invited into the Sergeants' Mess for a few bevvies, along with a Clearance Diver 1's course.

We were invited in because it was Trafalgar Night, always a big night in the Navy because of our, and indeed my, greatest ever hero, Lord Horatio Nelson. Trafalgar Night always managed to include drinking a copious amount of rum or grog. Grog is rum and water and was first introduced in 1756 for two reasons: to stop the sailor getting as drunk as he would on his neat rum, and to stop him hoarding it.

Eventually it all got just a little bit out of hand when we started the 'Trafalgar Olympics'. We played a few of our games, then they came up with a game they play in their mess, called the 'Cresta Run'. I'd never heard of it, apart from of course the winter games, which involves tearing down an ice course on something that resembles a tea tray.

In the mess they had a long polished antique-looking table that would probably seat 30 diners or more. They placed a soft blanket on the table and explained the idea behind the competition. What you had to do was take as long a run-up as you liked and, hurtling down the mess, launch yourself into the air and land on the blanket, skidding as far as you could along the table toboggan style; hence the 'Cresta Run'. Whoever can slide the furthest is the winner. There are of course all sorts of variables that can affect your glide distance, including some you find out the hard way – like if you jump too high, you come down too hard and don't travel the maximum distance; if you are heavy, you have greater momentum; if you are light, greater agility and acceleration. Also, I discovered, the smaller area you had in contact with the table, the less friction and the better glide you enjoyed. They gave us the opportunity to practise. Being all pretty fit, we saw this as right up our street. Fully grown men, running full tilt and flying through the air onto a blanket? Who invents such games?

Each distance was marked by a glass on the side of the table, until it was beaten, with the eventual furthest taking the prize. Having a bottle of rum as the prize was an encouragement to the Navy, and pushed all the competitors to ever greater endeavours. Ned Kelly, one of the divers, was winning at the time with a fantastically long leap. (Ned was a lovely bloke who later died in a tragic diving accident at Horsea Island.)

Nobby, during all of this, was quietly getting drunk, and was standing by the side of the table with a bit of a wobble on. The Mess Sergeant, a huge barrel-chested man, was determined to beat Ned's record distance. He came tearing down the hall and took off on his leap of faith.

Nobby then pulled his master stroke. Whilst the Sergeant was in mid-air, he grabbed the blanket and whipped it out of the way matador style, shouting 'Olé!'

The Sergeant of course now had no soft blanket to land on and nothing to slide on. His buttons scratched a deep groove in the ancient table and his face slammed down bringing him to a halt, ripping the skin off of his bottom lip and bloodying his nose. It made a noise not unlike a short skid from a car's tyres, but this was human flesh on varnished oak. Ouch! Nobby told me he just thought, 'Oh dear, he looks angry.' Well, he fucking well was angry. He rolled off the table and, even with his injuries, sought justice, and went in search of the matador. He took a swing at Nobby, who even in his drunken stupor saw it coming and did what anyone would do with enough warning – he ducked. The force of the Sergeant's momentum carried him right through his now prone target and another chief diver, Terry, who was stood behind Nobby, caught the punch square in the face. Terry, a quite innocent bystander, took umbrage at being hit by a man with whom he had recently been passing pleasantries, and hit him back. It soon developed into a typical bar-room brawl, only it was Army verses Navy, becoming our very own EOD equivalent of the annual Twickenham Battle.

I wonder if Nelson ever had such an incident after celebrating some distant victory. Interesting concept; celebrate a battle, with a battle.

Barrack Orphans

Barrack Orphan: *(definition)* A secretive lifeform that spends much of its time living and working undetected among larger populations of *Homo Militariens*. Blending in well, their presence in any colony or social group becomes detectable only at weekends and leave periods. At these times it is customary for members of the host community to leave the workplace and cluster in family groups, with families also clustering in territorial groups known as 'patches'. Unattached individuals usually migrate back to their places of origin, sometimes following tenuous social links for hundreds of miles to the place they were spawned. This leaves the base location with small pockets of infestation, now easily recognised as members of the *Saddus Illegitime* family and commonly known as 'Barrack Orphans'.

Their genus is divided into several subgroups, according to social state or motivation:

Simplex: Those with little or no remaining parental links: either true orphans in the conventional sense or, increasingly, children of divorced parents who prefer to avoid involvement in any subsequent acrimonious inter-parental exchanges.

Outcasticus: Those exhibiting sufficient antisocial characteristics to have been disowned by parents and friends. Members of this subgroup also find it difficult to blend into their host community, and are easily the most detectable subgroup.

Economicus (or Impecunius): This subgroup may have the opportunity and social links required, but lack the financial resources needed for migration. They perpetuate this state by expending what little resources they have on attempts at recreational activities in the base location.

Some suspected subgroups may not be true members of the genus, as the characteristic behaviour traits are temporary in nature. Two examples of these minority elements are:

Peniculus: In this subgroup social interaction at or near the base location, especially when linked with mating rituals, results in temporary relocation of thought processes to an alternative part of the anatomy. This disrupts behaviour patterns, undermines decision-making ability and sometimes causes complete loss of reasoning power.

Fugitus: Members of this subgroup may be mistakenly classified as *outcasticus* but are distinguished by the temporary nature of their self-imposed exile from migratory destinations. Most are either *Fugitus Pugnasticus* (having experienced physical conflict with a larger, stronger individual or group at the home location, and wishing to avoid repetition), or *Fugitus Criminalicus* (either guilty or suspected of unlawful acts, and likely to be apprehended by authorities at the home location).

Little is known of the Barrack Orphan reproductive process. Early models postulated a monthly cycle, based on records that revealed cyclical peaks in infestation numbers. These theories were discredited when increased numbers were found to be almost exclusively from the *Economicus (Impecunius)* sub-group, usually occurring on the third weekend of each month.

Barrack Orphans have few natural predators, so numerical equilibrium is maintained by means of individuals eventually achieving complete integration into the *Homo Militariens* host community. However, during weekends and leave periods when left alone and exposed, members are particularly prone to cranial attacks from moth-like ideas of the Emperor Mong variety (see chapter on this phenomenon).

A shorter definition... **Barrack Orphans**: The sad bastards left in camp after everyone with somewhere or someone to go to (and the money to do it!) has gone.'

Hoover? Damn!

It is the nature of the barrack orphan to be out of pocket (Harry Skinters) by the third or fourth day of the month, usually due to having just paid back money borrowed in order to survive the previous month. This catastrophic financial chain of events is usually repeated each month until the said orphan is lucky enough to find himself on an operational tour to some desolate or far-flung place where even a seasoned barrack orphan would find it impossible to spend money, such as Iraq, Afghanistan or South Georgia (800 miles East of the Falklands). There he is usually able to clear his debts until, of course, he finds himself back in the downward economic spiral of Regimental life between operational tours!

In some ways the barrack orphan can be compared to your average junkie (minus the drugs of course); desperate enough for cash that he will do practically anything in order to obtain it.

The orphan has been known to do some very strange and many may say 'desperate' deeds for money!

Domestic chores are one of the commonest and simplest money-making tasks carried out by the orphan desperate for cash. Such tasks can include washing, drying and ironing an entire troop/platoons' post-exercise kit (a truly horrible task!), cleaning webbing and equipment, washing cars, mowing lawns in and around the married quarters, emptying their garbage, or even single-handedly cleaning entire barrack blocks ready for the next week's inspection! Really desperate orphans have even been caught by hierarchy selling their entire 1157 (personal clothing and equipment) in car boot sales and, more recently, on E-Bay!

One such orphan, who was regularly desperate for cash within the first few days of the month, was a Sapper known by the strange nickname of 'Musky'.

It was the first Saturday of a new month. Saturday afternoons being post-POETS Day (Piss Off Early Tomorrow's Saturday), everyone in the block was naturally lazing around in an attempt to recover enough to repeat the previous night's entertainment of beer, song and mayhem all over again!

L/Cpl 'Vic' Leaman was a jammy sod and a bit of an Arthur Daley, usually coming up with luxury items from nowhere on exercise. He had somehow managed to procure himself a corporal's single bunk/room and was relaxing on his pit in his bunk watching Saturday afternoon footie and sipping his favourite (okay second favourite to Guinness) liquid refreshment of Twinings Earl Grey tea.

There was a knock at his door.

The door-knocker was 'Musky', bottle of beer in one hand and (strangely, on a Saturday) a 'hoover' in the other! Not unlike a brownie or cub scout going from house to house in their search to find some unfortunate victim they could con into paying for a household chore or more to be carried out, Musky, it appeared, had been doing the same. He had little joy around the pad's patch (married quarters) in the morning so was now going from room to room, block to block offering his hoovering services for cash, or better, for beer!

Always one to help any of the lads out Vic took pity on this penniless orphan and gave the hoover man permission to vacuum out his bunk, promising payment for his efforts of a Yellow Handbag[5] upon completion and passing Vic's meticulous post-hoover inspection.

Sweating like a fat lass in cling film, Musky set to his domestic task, spurred on with thoughts of the promised yellow handbag in payment. The minutes passed, and Vic thought a rather professional-looking job of the floor had been done, as he glanced down from the match on the telly. "Mrs Musky would be very proud of the fine job done by her offspring", he said, as Musky was now hoovering the rest of the room, window sills, light fittings, chairs, the table and had moved stealthily on to the top of Vic's lockers.

Suddenly, above the noise of the footie on the box, a roar was heard from the hoover as it strained to suck some unseen object into its hungry belly. This was followed by the very strange and somewhat disturbing sound of "Thwuuumph!" as it succeeded. Some unknown object had been sucked up inside! Musky's hysterical laughter followed these strange sounds. "What the Fuck was that?" asked Vic as he stood up and stared threateningly at Musky, who was laughing so hard he had lost the ability to speak and could only point. Vic followed Musky's hasty target indication and realised in utter horror what the strange sounds must have been, and what had now reduced Musky to a laughing, tear drenched idiot!

---

[5] The Yellow Handbag was at one time the most popular item sold by NAAFI in Germany. The ten pack of Herforder Pils contained in a yellow cardboard box with a convenient fold-out handle was just the right size to be stowed in side bins, under seats and a million and one other places in all manner of military vehicles. It was also seen on the way to parties and BBQs all over BFG (British Forces Germany), making the yellow handbag the ideal companion at work and play, also known to be the only 'handbag' in existence that any British Soldier would willingly and rather proudly, carry around in public.

"Timmy!" shouted Vic in desperation, tears welling and a lump in his throat as he stared helpless at the now empty goldfish tank that a minute before had been the comfortable home of his prized possession and trusted room companion – Timmy the Tamasaba Goldfish (one of the rarest and most expensive goldfish on the Planet!).

Like a man possessed, Vic grabbed the hoover and summoning immense strength (as only one whose life, or someone close to them, is immediately threatened, can), Vic ripped the hoover to pieces in his desperation to get to the dust bag inside. Finding it, he ripped it open, emptying the dusty, foul smelling contents all over the room in his blind panic. There on the floor, covered in dust, pubes, fag butts, soggy tissue, beer bottle tops and ring pulls, was a struggling Timmy. "He's alive!" screamed Vic, and with tears of joy he scooped his expensive and very rare mate up off the floor, returning him to his watery home.

Eventually, after several minutes, Musky regained the ability to speak. He apologised profusely to Vic, swearing that he had only meant to hoover up all the crap floating on the top of the tank (fish food and not so cheap tropical plants!), when probably out of curiosity Timmy had swum a bit too close to the hoover nozzle and had been unceremoniously vacuumed up along with his lunch and tropical plants.

"I didn't do it on purpose!" said Musky, as he sheepishly left through the door being held open by Vic, head down, bag of hoover bits and pieces in one hand and yellow handbag conspicuously absent from the other.

Timmy the Tamasaba Goldfish survived with no physical injuries, but for the remainder of his days no doubt suffered with PTSD (in this case, Post Traumatic owned by a Squaddie Disorder)!

5.   On the Move

Overseas deployments bring a charm all their own to operations and exercises alike. Squaddies relish the challenge of practising their roles in a new environment, among people of different cultures and, for some best of all, many miles from the influences and limitations of home. This usually means trouble.

Got a Fag Mate?

We did an UNFICYP (United Nations Forces in Cyprus) tour in 1976-77 and spent two weeks in the Box Factory somewhere near Ay Nick at the eastern end of the Green Line near the ESBA. Being an abandoned box factory, it was full of cardboard boxes (no surprise there, then) which meant that smoking inside was prohibited.

There was a circuit round the factory for the scout cars. The Troop Sergeant's driver came in from patrol and disappeared round the corner out of the way for a quick drag and came back looking puzzled. Jock proceeded to recount how he'd been pulling hard on a Regal when a voice came across the open ground from the Turkish trenches not that many meters away (though I never saw them). The voice asked, in broad Cockney, if he might have a fag, mate.

Jock looks around, baffled, then espies a Turkish helmet. Supposedly not talking to the combatants we were supposed to be keeping apart, but out of sight anyway, Jock asks WTF?

Cockney announces that he was from Kensington way and a loyal Chelsea supporter, but half Turkish and when he'd travelled over to visit his father on holiday, they'd been about to invade, he was conscripted and had spent the last eighteen months in the trench. And could he have a fag, mate – please?

Sideboards and the Senior Warrant Officer

Three Young Sappers were walking along what was the longest continuous wooden corridor in the world (the Death Star, more commonly known as Mount Pleasant Airfield, Falkland Islands) with the intention of eating in the Crab mess hall and looking forward to the delights of full roast beef, lobster thermidor or elvers with lemon sole followed by what can only be described as the largest cheese board south of the equator, not to mention as many helpings of strawberries with cream or ice cream sundae as they could get down their necks! The delights of the lower Army cookhouse could be endured for just so long; daily portions of cheese possessed toasties with a soggy piece of pineapple on top, or babies' heads and gravy with mashed potato made out of a packet. The use of compo rations and fresh mixture was a fine art in the Army cookhouse, in fact the cooks were so good at it they didn't even need any 'fresh' to mix with the compo!

Many say SAS Selection isn't actually the hardest course in the British Army, and claim that honour goes to the Army catering course, as it is obvious no one has ever passed the fucker! Army Privates of all units would stash their berets inside their combat jackets and sneak undetected (most of the time) into the RAF restaurant (mess hall). This was a traditional once a week luxury our hapless three had indulged in for the previous two months.

About 100m short of the target (RAF Cordon Bleu Restaurant with two Michelin Stars) the three Sappers were shocked to attention by the booming command of, "You three – HAAAALT RIGHT THERE!" Our intrepid three suddenly found themselves face to face with a small barrel of an RAF Station Warrant Officer (kind of like an RSM, and almost equally ferocious) who, red-faced, pointed his pace-stick in the face of Sapper JB (a six foot four, not-so-bright sprog of a Sapper from the Lowlands of Scotland) and growled out the words "You are Sappers aren't you! Tell me, young man, what exactly do Army Regulations say about sideboards?" Young Sapper JB was himself sporting sideboards that any character from a Dickens novel would have been be proud to own. He thought for a few seconds and then said, "Well, Sir, you don't *have* to have them."

The Station Warrant Officer was rendered speechless, stick hovering in mid–air as the happy three continued on their way.

Going Up in the World

Those who served in Northern Ireland during the early 1980s may remember the construction projects to build mortar-proof bases at Forkhill and Crossmaglen. Royal Engineers carried out the construction, reinforced by Royal Pioneer Corps elements, but many more will remember the resupply operations.

Deep in 'bandit country', routine movements in and out of these bases was by helicopter. Heavy stores and aggregate had to be transported by road, however, and once every three or four months it took a major security effort to safely meet project requirements. All high-risk counter-terrorist search teams in Province became involved, clearing the planned resupply routes, while around twelve companies of Infantry provided OPs and patrols to secure the routes during clearance and the subsequent convoy movements. It paid to get the project 'shopping-list' right; there would be a three to four month wait for any omissions.

This story centres on the Crossmaglen base, where space was so tight that a tower crane was the only effective way to move stores and components around the construction site. Components for the tower crane had been delivered and assembled, but it needed to be inspected and formally commissioned by a civilian representative of the crane company before being used. The Sappers responsible for that phase of construction – 1 Troop, 9 Parachute Squadron RE – welcomed the company representative on his arrival at the Crossmaglen base and the unit crane operators all joined him to assist with the inspection.

All went well until the final phase...

The crane stood twenty or thirty feet higher than the cover-from-view fence and the intention was to operate it remotely from the ground. However, the final phase of inspection needed the Inspector and an assistant up on the crane gantry to control and observe components during activation.

When he asked for a volunteer to help with this, the inspector was surprised to see the crane operators all looking at each other with raised eyebrows and signs of nervousness.

"Come on, guys," he encouraged, "I didn't expect you Paras to be scared of heights!"

At this point the senior crane operator, a full-screw, stepped forward and with a fatalistic shrug said, "Oh, well – I suppose this is where I earn my stripes."

They had been up on the gantry, exposed well above the cover from the cover-from-view fence, for less than three minutes when shots rang out. The inspector began to scream and clutched at his thigh, where blood had begun to flow freely. The full-screw disconnected his safety harness, hurried to the inspector and cradled him down to ground level. The CASEVAC operation went smoothly, and the wounded civvy was soon treated, safe and recovering in the hospital at Aldergrove. The full-screw remained in Crossmaglen, shaken but not stirred.

The Sapper Squadron OC went to visit the inspector in hospital the following day and was relieved to find that the wound was not too serious; he'd been caught by either a ricochet or metal splinter, rather than a direct hit.

"I feel a bit of a prat!" said the Inspector. "How stupid was I not to realize why your crane ops were nervous about sticking heads, arses and everything in between above the cover-from-view fence. I was also a bit of a tit for screaming so much when the wound wasn't all that serious." He asked that his apology and sincere thanks be passed to the crane ops, especially the corporal who had brought him down, and went on to say he'd be pleased to return and complete the inspection as soon as he was able.

The OC promised to pass on the message, though he pointed out that it was both understandable and a good sign if you could still scream after being shot. He also asked whether there was anything he could do for the Inspector. Sheepishly, the Inspector asked, "Could you phone my wife, and tell her where I am?" The OC offered to bring a phone to his bed, at which he blushed even deeper and stuttered "No, no! You don't understand ... I need *you* to tell her. I thought she'd worry, so I didn't tell her I was coming to Northern Ireland. She thinks I'm in Scotland!"

We never got to meet his wife, so we'll assume it was a comment on marriage in general that he was perfectly willing to return and face the snipers again, but couldn't summon up the courage to explain to his wife!

Burning the Trash in Style

I was with 88 Battery, 4 Regiment RA and had spent the previous week in Romeo Tower on Camlough Mountain. The unit taking over, 2 Battalion, Royal Green Jackets, had sent a team up on the mountain to replace us.

We'd bagged all the rubbish from our stint and stashed it ready for pickup by the helicopter. We were airlifted down to the mill and then after a shower and feeding, straight out onto a twelve-hour PVCP shift by the church and RUC station.

We'd briefed the oncoming team that the rubbish was to go out on a helicopter, NOT burned, but they thought they knew better. The wind got up, burning rubbish got into the grass and caused a pretty nasty fire. We were watching from the PVCP through binos as they tried to beat the fire out and then started running like fuck when they realised that the claymores were going to blow.

There was a lot of chortling in the Ops Room that night as the reports came in of the resulting explosions but I never did find out what happened to the soldiers concerned.

Green Light Go

In Aden during the very early 1960s one young RAF electrician was given the job of wiring in the jump lights on a Beverley for a visiting unit of the Parachute Regiment so that they could do a jump. The Beverley has two floors. Anyway, said electrician sets up the jump lights and checks they work etc. – job done.

The following day the Beverley sets off with a full complement of Paras ready to do a tactical jump. As the Beverley starts its approach the pilot sets the top deck light to amber standby. Unbeknownst to anyone, the RAF electrician has cross-wired the lights and the bottom deck goes immediately green. Paras on the bottom deck think "Hmm...Crabs have forgotten the amber..." and begin throwing themselves from the aircraft – over the ocean!

The Crew Chief spots what's happening and immediately informs the pilot, who flicks the switch back, but a green light comes up on the top deck. Paras on the top deck are ready to go, and... Well, to cut a long story short, the RAF electrician spends the rest of his time there keeping a low profile from a group of ticked-off Paras who all landed in the 'oggin'.

(And if there are any of that group reading this – my Dad says sorry!)

A Bit of a Dump

During the late 1970s in Belize, what eventually became Battlegroup South was little more than a patrol base. A Sapper troop was sent to improve living conditions and early addition was a deep trench latrine. Due to ground conditions and copious tree roots, this was excavated double width and a felled tree trunk positioned along the centre of its length for support. Users had the option of a 'laid-back dump' (feet against the trench edge, small of the back against the tree trunk) or a 'hangover' (upper thighs sitting on the tree trunk, with rear end hanging over the far side of the trench). Seem obvious enough?

A few days after the latrine had entered use, the Infantry CSM was checking defensive positions during the evening Stand To and discovered that an infantryman was absent from his trench. "Where's Murphy?" he asked the section commander, and was told, "Went for a dump just before Stand To, Sir!" Rather than disrupt the outer perimeter, he asked the Sapper section commander to send one of his men to fetch Murphy, but five minutes later the Sapper hadn't returned. Stand To ended and the Sapper section commander went to investigate. He found his man sitting against a tree near the latrine, laughing uncontrollably and weakly pointing towards the trench. Approaching the trench, the section commander began to understand why the retrieval task was taking longer than expected. Murphy was squatting at the bottom of the trench, trousers lowered and up to his fifth lace-holes in the slurry the trench was designed for.

"I can see what you're doing, Murphy, but why are you doing it down there?" asked the corporal.

"Well, I thought you'd know. The past few days I'd been thinking youze Sappers had dug this thing much too deep, and only made it usable by adding the log."

Suppressing his own laughter, and doing his best to look serious, the Corporal asked, "Then why didn't you use the log, like everybody else?"

"Sure, I have done every time," replied Murphy. "How else do you think I've been climbing out?"

King-size Flies

I remember 9 Parachute Squadron, Royal Engineers digging the world's most horrible shite pit, outside the footy stadium in Kigali, Rwanda. They stuck a 9 x 9 over it with three wooden traps, separated by a bit of hessian.

It was alright for a week or so, but after a while it really started to stink. People kept wazzing all over the seats. It was more pungent than a pungent bag of really pungent things!

There was a big sign saying "Please put the lid down after you have finished" but nobody bothered and the flies turned up in force. After a couple of generations they started to get really big, which was not surprising, living down there amongst the world's biggest supply of bluebottle-nectar.

When the lids were down they were trapped in the dark, but as soon as you lifted one and sat down, a few of them would make a break for it. Most would just bounce off your arse, which felt like being punched by a midget. After we'd been there a couple of months one of them escaped while I was in trap one. It flew up through the gap between my legs. It was fucking enormous! It looked like a rolled up army sock with wings. I just sat there, horrified as it clambered out and fell off my knee on to the deck. It was a right fat bastard and had used up all its energy getting past my balls.

Eventually, after it got its breath back, it walked off towards the cookhouse. Sitting there, I had one of those 'philosophical' moments. We eat there and shit here. They eat here and...

No – It doesn't bear thinking about!

What a Tosser

It was 1997 at Salmon Range, Bosnia, somewhere in the hills between Gornji Vakuf and Novi Travnik. We were a four-man Royal Engineer EOD Team and had been destroying all sorts of nice items in our designated demolition pit for the past couple of hours and were nearing completion of the day's task.

We were left with the final serial of the day, which was approximately 1500 Yugoslavian M52 hand grenades which we had previously stripped down, checked and put back together (in certain areas of Bosnia the M52 had been turned into a booby trap, which worked by releasing the striker immediately the pin was pulled, rather than initiating a short delay as the fly-off lever separated from the grenade upon throwing). Thanks to stripping and checking, we knew we had 1500 primed and non-booby-trapped grenades to 'destroy' and all agreed the best way to Mag to Grid (get rid) the said items was to pull the pins and throw them.

After years of destroying thousands of items of ordnance in the demolitions pit it was now over 10m in diameter and 5m deep. We simply picked up a grenade each from the back of the MPV (Mine Protected Vehicle) and dressed off a metre or so back from the edge of this massive dems pit. On the word of command we all pulled our pins, lobbed the four grenades at a time underarm into the bottom of the pit and walked back a safe distance until all four grenades went off. We repeated this for the next hour or so, thus saving on the plastic explosive needed to destroy the items the 'conventional' way. Plastic explosive was at a premium, after all.

All went swimmingly and we were down to the last few grenades when Sapper 'Harry' (one of our two drivers and not long out of training) turned to the Team Commander and said, "Hey Sarn't, I was sick during the grenade lessons in training and was the only one not to have thrown on the grenade range. I've still never thrown one as it's supposed to be thrown [you know – pull the ring with attached pin from grenade, ring with pin held close to the chest, grenade body with fly-off lever held securely and at arm's length before shouting out loudly 'GRENADE!' and then lobbing over-arm said weapon towards the enemy]. Any chance of having a go now? Go on... please?"

Bill, our Sergeant, Team Commander and Bomb Disposal Officer turned to me as the Team Corporal.

"What do you think? I don't personally see any harm in it."

I thought for all of two seconds then said, "Bloody great 10m diameter and 4m deep hole to throw the grenade into from 15m back close to the MPV under our supervision? I don't see why not, Bill as there can't be anyone in NATO, let alone anywhere else, who could possibly miss a target like that!"

"My thoughts exactly Al. Okay, Harry... pick yourself one of the last of the grenades out of the vehicle then stand beside me over here and I'll take you through it."

So there we were – Bill with Harry 3m ahead of me and Eddie the other Sapper driver. Bill talks Harry through the drill one last time. Harry, with his green ball of death and destruction clutched close to his chest, looks around at the three of us, sporting what can only be described as the stupidest grin in the Balkans (or anywhere else, come to that). He then proceeds to correctly pull the body of the grenade away from the ring and pin and with an almighty "GRENAAADE!" proceeds to lob said grenade over-arm, supposedly towards the 'Grand Canyon' to his front.

We were all looking expectantly towards the 'Grand Canyon' of a demolitions pit 15m away, prepared for the last sight of the grenade heading on its final journey into the pit of doom, when Schhhhhhhhhhhhplup! The grenade comes flying back down and lands right where the four of us are standing!

"FaaaAAARK!"

Split-second instinct took over. I ran straight at Eddie, throwing him and myself behind the giant wheel of the MPV and a split second later Sapper Harry was lifted clean off his feet by the pint-sized Sarn't Bill. Like two heavy sacks of spuds they thudded down on top of us, squashing us into the snow and mud at exactly the same time as the almighty explosion from the grenade, which went off no more than 3m away from us all! Luckily the MPV took the entire brunt of the blast and frag. The only injury sustained was Sapper Harry's bruising from the thwacking that followed from the other three of us!

When we all sat up and realized everyone was okay, we did what any other squaddie would have done in the same situation. As one we burst out laughing, though more from relief than anything else! The damage to the armoured glass and other parts of the MPV took a bit of explaining, and poetic license played a big part in our escape from repercussions.

A Painful Pre-dick-ament

We were in Cyprus on Exercise PINESTICK 1995 with 11 Field Squadron Royal Engineers. On one of many nights out in Akrotiri we met up with a netball team doing a tour of the Island. One of the lads' (Sapper Staples) party pieces was to use drawing pins to stick his foreskin to a bar table and then drag said table along the floor a few metres, much to the 'delight' of whoever was watching at the time. Tonight he was looking forward to having an entire sexy netball team as his enthusiastic audience.

Having performed this feat many times before, Sapper Staples had no fear of failure but on this occasion he had unfortunately overlooked a couple of important details. Not only was the table bolted to the floor but also the bar floor had recently been mopped and was still wet and slippery...

After a suitable introduction, Sapper Staples proceeded to get out his cock and well-stretched foreskin, then produced a handful of large drawing pins, just as he had done on many a previous 'party piece' occasion. Then, much to the delight of the admiring netball players, he picked out one lucky lady from the crowd to do the delicate deed and even helped her push the drawing pins all the way down. What happened next would make a large crowd of grown men cry. It even reduced a female netball team to screaming, fainting wrecks!

With hands on hips, and after several winks and smiles at the female audience, Sapper Staples took the strain, not dissimilar to your average tug-of-war team. He then took a confident step backwards, fully expecting the table to move with him from its place on the bar floor. Instead, he slipped on the wet floor and his legs flew out from under him. Gravity took over. With the table bolted firmly in place and his foreskin well and truly pinned to the tabletop, there could be only one outcome...

An eye-watering, gut-wrenching, ripping sound split the air in the bar, closely followed by a loud, drawn-out scream of pain from Sapper Staples and shrieks of shock and horror from the mainly female audience. Several fainted (not just the ladies!), legs were convulsively crossed (not just the men!) and there seemed to be split foreskin and blood everywhere.

After Sapper Staples' colleagues amongst the audience had stopped pissing themselves laughing and uncrossed their legs, we had a collective serious attack. Emergency services were called, an ambulance arrived and Sapper Staples was quickly carted off to the nearby military hospital.

"How on earth did you do this?" asked the duty nurse to Sapper Staples in the hospital.

"I caught me foreskin in me flies in the loo," came Sapper Staples' weak reply.

"I don't think so," replied the nurse.

"Eh? Why's that then?" asked Sapper Staples.

"Well, call me a bluff old traditionalist, but you are wearing button-up Levi 501s, Dickhead!" came the duty nurse's quick-witted reply.

Are You Going to Take That Lying Down?

When we were on the Rwanda operation in 1994, we tried to pilfer a load of American camp-cots.

There were eight of us in our room, but only two of us had the Yank items. Everyone else had British 'tarantula sanctuaries' – two inches off the deck until you got your fat arse on them, then the only thing separating you from the floor was 3mm of dry, urine-infused canvas.

Something had to be done. URFA and I took it upon ourselves to conduct a Robin Hood escapade to rob from the rich (Americans) and give to the poor (us lot). We took a half-ton Landrover to Kigali airport and had a snoop around. Within a couple of minutes we'd spotted a yank truck full of the fuckers (camp cots, that is!). We backed the rover up and helped ourselves to the six required, then looked at each other and had the same thought. 'Convoy and URFAs Camp-Cot Emporium' supplying superior bedding to tramps like us, for knockdown prices. We were having a right giggle at our top quality thievery, and the back of the rover was nearly full when a fucking big master sergeant, showed up and said,

"Hey! What the fuck are you guys doing?"

We immediately dropped into the standard kids' response. We looked at our shoes and said, "Nothing."

"You mutha-fuckers taking cots?"

Very quietly, still looking at feet, "Yes."

"Shee-it boys, help yo-fuckin' selves! They be doin no mutha-fucker no fucking good in the back o' that machine. Take as many as you need."

But it was 'shee-it' after that. We didn't really want the cots. We were only enjoying the nicking. Where was the fun if he was letting us have them? He'd spoiled it, the bastard! We got a few and drove off. Fortunately for us, it was a ten-minute drive back to the camp. This gave us ample time to fabricate a story, which involved a 'Smokey and the Bandit' style car chase across the pan, ending with the Master Sergeant fading in to our rearview mirror, shaking his fist, shouting, "I'll get dem pesky Limeys if it's the last thing I do!"

Blackout at Byron Heights

I was a young Sapper on my first Operational Tour back in 1987 in the Falkland Islands; we were a Combat Engineer Section and were tasked with building concrete paths leading in and around one of the RAF Radar Domes on top of the mountain "Byron Heights" on West Falklands.

The RAF were so anal about their bloody Dome that we were never allowed to view inside it. It was one of the early warning radars to detect enemy aircraft approaching the Falkland Islands, hence the reason the RAF in their wisdom didn't allow our 'planners' to view too much of the blueprint of the mountain-top site!

Most of the time, we were in the clouds, piss-wet through. It was like working non-stop in a fog bank that had somehow been transported through time and space 8,000 miles south from the River Thames and Charles Dickens' or Jack the Ripper's London of the 1800s! Whenever we had the 'pleasure' of an interval between the soggy 'Whitechapel' fog banks we would be constantly harassed by the dreaded 'Kara-Kara' – whopping great big 'birds of prey'! (yes, their name does sound suspiciously similar to *hara-kiri* although their suicidal tendencies more closely resembled the *kamikaze* suicide dive-bombing squads from WWII. But these beasts were worse; not only would they survive each attack, they would come back for revenge almost straight away!)

The Kara-Kara were sneaky bastards, trying to befriend you in the morning by winking, smiling and nodding at you as if in some weird 'ornithological' way they were saying "Good morning fellas, we hope you'll put up a better fight today!"

The Kara-Kara's 'attack at all cost' instincts against anyone in a British uniform were so well-honed that we had our suspicions they had been the Argentinean Army's household pet equivalent of our budgerigar or parrot and were now avenging their long-gone owners! It didn't pass our thoughts either that they might well have been a secretly trained 'feathered army' that were now spear-heading some kind of elaborate Top Secret contingency plan thought up by a clever Argentinean Commander to drive all British Forces from the Falkland Islands.

These creatures could have fitted in quite easily alongside their ancestors in the Hitchcock film *The Birds*. They would wait until we had our hands full, carrying bags of cement or large rocks we had 'quarried' earlier from the chain-gang rock face, before dive-bombing us, always from behind and at a rate of knots! The only warning was a resounding, suicidal cry of *"Kara-KaraaaAA!"* a split-second before unceremoniously crashing into our heads or necks! The only thing these feathered fuckers were missing was a Rising Sun emblazoned on strips of cloth, tied bandana-style round their bald little heads! But enough of the wildlife ... on with the story!

We were working out in the elements for nine or ten hours a day, constantly soaked to the skin by either the 'soggy Thames fog bank' or by the sweat of the day's hard labour, and much of the time by both! The fucking Navvies who built the railroads through the Wild West had it easier than us; at least they had the use of explosives to break their rock up for them. For the first four weeks, I kid you not, we had only sledgehammers and pickaxes to break the rock down into sizeable rock-crusher machine 'friendly' sized lumps in order to make our own aggregate for the concrete.

Our squadron wouldn't give us any rock breakers from the G1098 stores back at Mount Pleasant Airfield as they had just been cleaned and oiled prior to the OC's Inspection and were to take pride of place in the Station Commander's inspection after that! As any good British Empire Medal winning military storeman will tell you 'stores are for storing'! The phrase 'like getting blood from a stone' was quite literal in our case! It was to be a month before we were to see our rock breakers and generators appear from the back of a Chinook helicopter and it could only be compared to a young lad getting his first ever Action Man for Christmas!

One afternoon I was building the formwork for one of the concrete paths out of railway sleepers and keeping it in place with two-foot metal pickets every couple of feet or so (we sledgehammered the pickets into the ground to stop the formwork moving when we poured the concrete). All hell suddenly broke loose. Bear in mind that it was an extremely rare occurrence to catch a fleeting glimpse of one of the RAF bods appearing outside the dome they reputedly manned. On the extremely rare occasions that we had this pleasure, it would usually be no more than a blur of RAF blue travelling at the speed of a gazelle between the containerized, windowless accommodation and office complex to the radar dome or vice-versa. It was on these very rare occasions that we realized the RAF weren't actually as unfit as we all thought they were. When you did actually catch a frame of them as they 'blurred' past, it was as if you had caught a moment right out of Scott of the Antarctic's Expedition to the South Pole – we had no idea there was so much arctic kit available in the stores of the British Armed Forces, let alone handed out to one person!

For us it was a breath of fresh air to behold one of these Blue Jobs as it confirmed to us that the Mountain Top Radar Outpost wasn't just inhabited nightly by the 'RAF Drinking and Singing Team' as the only time we seemed to see any of them was after work at night, when amazingly the bar would be bursting at the seams with them! We had almost convinced ourselves that the radar was run remotely from some secret hotel on West Falklands and this 'Drinking and Singing Team' was being dropped off silently around 1800 hours each evening then equally silently extracted in the early hours back to their luxury seaside hotel to sleep during the day!

Back to this particular afternoon, destined to become infamous for a story to be told and retold to thousands who visited the mountain-top site for years to come (I know this to be true, as I returned as a Lance Corporal Section 2IC a few years later to build a flexible diesel pipeline – 8 kilometres to the pumping site at Whale Cove – but that's another story!).

Suddenly, from every crack and orifice in the outpost appeared a countless swarm of RAF personnel: radar workers, technicians, chefs, mechanics and signallers, all running around the mountain-top, screaming and yelling like headless chickens. In fact, there were so many of them running around that you could have been forgiven for thinking you were actually at Biggin Hill at the height of the Battle of Britain during WWII! All that was missing was the air raid sirens and a distorted voice crackling "Bandits approaching, ten o'clock high!" from a Tannoy system.

We had no idea what was happening until a few minutes later, when a reincarnation of Scott of the Antarctic and his entire crew came running over to where our section was working. We then had an idea something was 'up', and it slowly dawned on me that *I* may well be the cause of all this mayhem. A minute earlier, as I had hammered another picket, there had been 'a bit of a bang' and I was covered in some foul-smelling smoke from the hole the picket had made in the ground... I hadn't thought anything of it at the time, suspecting I may have put the metal picket through some kind of large calibre round that was buried there. I suppose I must actually have thought, somewhere at the back of my mind, that it might have been 'something else', as I did loosen the picket with a wooden pick helve prior to pulling it out of the ground to reposition it.

I had just pulled the said picket out of the ground when Scott and his crew appeared in front of me, looking none-too-pleased as I stood there, with a one-foot picket in hand that a minute ago had been a two-foot picket, in the middle of a slowly clearing, acrid cloud of smoke – smoke that smelled suspiciously like burning electrical cable and was clearly coming from the picket-shaped hole in the ground! It was a feeling not too dissimilar to being a small kid who has just been caught hand-in-jar at the local corner sweet shop!

It turned out that I had hammered the picket through the underground electric cable that provided the radar and the entire outpost's power – all 50,000 volts of it! Mass panic had erupted through the outpost as all the monitor screens suddenly blacked out, along with the rest of the electrical equipment. I had single-handedly disabled one of the world's best early warning systems, allowing any Argentinean aircraft that fancied their chances that day to slip stealthily below the radar. Luckily for me, there were none about to exploit this window of opportunity!

Some good did come of the epic event. As the cable was repaired, the Blue Jobs managed to finish watching whatever porn film they'd been halfway through and our Section Commander was shown the blueprint of every tiny intricate part of the Mountain Top. The path was moved several metres to the south and we retired early that day to the depths of the accommodation complex.

That evening the silently inserted 'RAF Drinking and Singing Team' appeared to quadruple in size, probably due to the two crates of 'Red' (McEwans) and two crates of 'Green' (Heineken) beer I was charged with providing as the penalty awarded by a hastily convened kangaroo court after work!

From that day forth we got on 'spiffingly' with the fine men of Her Majesty's Royal Air Force. Many a can of 'Red' or 'Green' (and on special occasions of 'Blue' Fosters) were drunk, and tales of derring-do told with our new-found friends the 'Boys in Blue'. When our construction task was completed we had the send-off of all send-offs from the mountain on our final night – at times even managing to out-sing the RAF 'Drinking & Singing Team' with renditions of their own gozzome Song 'The Wokka-Wokka'.

As our parting gift we presented the Station/Outpost Commander with a precisely scaled miniature model of the entire mountain top, including radar dome, and even a miniature set of Arctic goggles on Scott of the Antarctic rushing between dome and accommodation complex.

It was so detailed that anyone subjecting the model to really close scrutiny could make out a tiny 'picket-like' metal pin protruding from a certain spot not far from the radar dome.

6. Out of Africa

As mentioned in the introduction to the previous chapter, all overseas deployments have a charm of their own, but Africa is a place apart, so deserves a chapter to itself. Besides, the chapter title had a certain ring to it... can't think why.

Mountaineering Mayhem

It was the early/mid 1990s in Kenya. We were a four-man Sapper Expedition team and had spent the past week on Mount Kenya, Africa's second highest mountain at 5,199m (17,058 feet). It is a fascinating mountain, snow-capped and with glaciers, even though it lies on the Equator. The first European to discover this fact, Johann Ludwig Krapf (1810-81) was ridiculed by the 'experts' back home in Europe, who may well have coined the phrase 'talking a load of Krapf'. It had been a memorable week, and we were happy to add to the wealth of tales already told about the mountain.[6]

The unexpected weight of our bergens had been due mainly to the ten-man ration packs the QM of 3 Para had issued to us a week earlier, with a very large grin on his face and the excuse, "Sorry lads, we can't spare 'boil in the bag' rat packs for Adventure Training". He had a point though, and we were happy enough to have been given any rations from the stores. The week spent humping these loads up and then back down the mountain had taken its toll. Suffice it to say we were exhausted and in need of plenty of scoff and a good night's kip by the time

---

[6] One of the most amusing happened during WWII, when it was climbed by three Italian Prisoners of War who had escaped from the British POW Camp at Nanyuki. They made a valiant attempt on the highest peak of the mountain and managed to reach almost 17,000ft, where they planted their Italian Flag in defiance and then 'escaped' back into the camp! See the book "No Picnic on Mount Kenya" to read their story.

we reached the Weather/Met Station at 10,000ft on the Naro Moru route.

We'd managed to get up the mountain and back down almost unscathed, though I still carry a scar to this day on my head. While climbing a particularly steep part of the mountain, I needed all four points of contact on the rock. I heard a strange grating sound a moment before the rock face (after staying quite happily where it was for 2.5 billion years) decided that during the 20 seconds I happened to be clinging onto it would be a good time to take a trip down the mountainside! Thankfully, my belaying buddy managed to save the day and I only fell about 30 feet, but I was almost knocked unconscious in the fall. (If you are unfortunate enough to be reading this book, Jim – thanks mate!).

The only other disfigurements the team brought back were the mental scars of being traumatized by one of the strangest animals on Planet Earth – a small, furry mammal called the Rock Hyrax. These look like robust, oversized guinea pigs or rabbits with rounded ears and no tail. They have stumpy toes with hoof-like nails, four toes on each front foot and three on each back foot. The longer, claw-like nails on the inside toes of the back feet are used for grooming and scratching. The bottoms of the feet have a rubbery texture to assist in climbing steep rock surfaces and trees. Apparently the closest relative to this creature is the elephant (hold on... Rock Hyrax: a foot-high cross between a gerbil and the Tasmanian Devil – Elephant: MASSIVE!)

Anyway, these little bastards kept us awake at Mackinder's Hut with their incessant growling, whistling and really annoying shrieking. This starts as a squeak or whistle, then rises to a pig-like squeal and finally to a scream, like a small child's tantrum! They also carry rabies, so we didn't want to get too close to them to ask if they would kindly 'shut the fuck up' at lights out!

Back down at the Met Station we managed to swap some of our remaining compo rations with local staff for three large loaves of delicious-looking, freshly-baked bread. They also very kindly pointed out some inviting-looking Swiss Alp style large cabins/bunkhouses at the edge of the nearby woodland and told us that if they were open, we could spend our final night on the mountain in comfort inside them. Brilliant! We would make an 'all-in' of our remaining curried chicken, tinned burgers and babies' heads (tinned individual steak and kidney puddings,) accompanied by our recently-acquired freshly-baked bread – and all in the comfort of a warm alpine hut to boot – Lovely Jubbly!

It was getting late in the evening as we wearily, but happily approached the mini alpine village. Our spirits soared as we heard the faint but familiar sounds of singing and laughter coming from the direction of the largest and only illuminated alpine hut. We knew what Frodo Baggins, Fat Sam, Merry and Pippin from the Lord of the Rings, must have felt as they neared the 'Prancing Pony' at Bree with its equally alluring sounds of merriment from within! We reached the door of the hut and the whole place was vibrating with the sounds from within; a mixture of laughter, song, happy shouts and what could only have been large beer steins being banged rhythmically on wooden tables in time to a song. The song and sounds were not dissimilar to the famous scene from *The Student Prince of Heidelberg*, dominated by the chorus of "Drink! Drink! Drink!"

Grinning like three Cheshire Cats, we knocked on the door, fully expecting shortly to be joining in the song and beer with the alpine hut's inhabitants – the Student Prince and his mates. After knocking louder and louder on the door, it became obvious that we couldn't be heard above the singing, shouting and laughter coming from within, so we opened the door and walked in.

Instead of the Student Prince and his Merry Mates we were greeted by the sight of around thirty elderly men and women sat around an enormous wooden table, which was in imminent danger of collapse under the weight of the medieval banquet and the family-sized beer steins perched on top of it! The singing and merriment ceased the instant we entered the room, not unlike the minute leading up to 'High Noon' in the classic Western. The two opposing sides stared at each other: the three of us in our tropical cammed trousers and British Army issue bergens (one of which was proudly flying a small Union Jack from a side pocket) staring back at more than thirty angry-looking faces. After the initial shocked silence, the largest amongst them stood up and spat out, "Zer iss no room in here for you – you muss leave ziss place immediately!" As much as we appreciated that the Germans had invented modern-day Christmas Festivities as we know them, there wasn't a virgin among us, so we didn't feel we deserved that most Biblical of all quotes ("Sorry, but there is no room at the Inn"). However, we realised that we had just gate-crashed what must have been the Fiftieth Gestapo Reunion! We got the point very quickly and made a sharp exit, counting ourselves lucky that we hadn't been mown down in a hail of Luger, Mauser and Walther PP bullets!

Licking our wounds, we sheepishly made our way back to the Weather Station, accompanied by gradually fading sounds of laughter from our 'Friends of ze Vaterland' within their alpine hut, where the chorus of "Drink! Drink! Drink!" had been resumed, although we wondered why anyone would need that much encouragement. By contrast, the eloquent silence at our end was screaming "Fucking Jerries!"

We arrived back at the weather station as darkness was setting in, so decided to spend the night in the shelter of a large concrete and wooden gazebo/summer house thing. A fire was lit in the centre of the gazebo, and we got out our doss bags to sit on. Then we pooled all our remaining rations together in a pile by the fire, leaving only a final brew-making kit and the prized boil-in-the-bag beans and sausages we had saved for our last day (proffed above and beyond our ten-man rat packs). We placed the brew kit and breakfast into one of the bergens.

Just as we had emptied the pooled rations into a couple of mess tins to make our all-in meal, and finished cutting up the delicious looking freshly baked bread – ALL HELL BROKE

LOOSE! As if by magic, hordes of massive black and white Sykes monkeys came charging into our small camp from all directions, screaming their mad war-cries. It had to have been planned as half of them attacked us while the other half peeled off and made bee-lines for the mess tins, bread, doss bags and bergens! Their initial 'planned' attack was over in seconds; everything had been grabbed and taken, apart from a solitary remaining loaf of bread.

When the war cries and shrieks disappeared into the darkness we edged out of the gazebo and found our bergens completely emptied out, kit scattered everywhere. The fuckers had even found our stashed breakfast and had ripped open all the packets and bags and munched the lot, including the tea bags. As if that wasn't bad enough, they had rubbed salt in the wounds by swamping on our Expedition Team Leaders' doss bag! We armed ourselves with some large sticks and defended our small encampment through the night, the "Sykes Monkey Mafia" attacked us a further five times over the next few hours. During a lull in the battle, we cut up our remaining loaf of bread and started to toast the slices, when two of our assailants literally leaped over the fire and grabbed all our half-toasted bread before disappearing laughing into the darkness!

Those fucking black and white bastards were to lay siege to us throughout the night. We were very grateful to see the 'cavalry' appear on the horizon below the weather station the following morning in the shape of a 4-ton truck that had arrived to pick us up.

Feeding Time at Archer's Post (a Kenyan Tale)

Archer's Post, Kenya – those who have been there can't easily forget the place. It's where the British Army carries out advanced live-firing exercises, usually as part of Exercise *Grand Prix*. It is a desolate, dusty, unforgiving place in the middle of nowhere. Some of the world's hottest temperatures have been recorded there over the years.

I was a Lance Jack in the Royal Engineers at the time and had arrived to take over the running of the water supply point for the camp. I was introduced to the 3 Para Assault Pioneer Platoon who would run the water point with me for the next week or so. There had been problems with turning the thick hot chocolate coloured water pumped from the wide river running next to the tented camp into potable water. A quick inspection of the Water Purification Unit (WPU) confirmed to me that the equipment must surely have been left behind by Lieutenant John Rouse Merriot Chard VC of the Royal Engineers when he and his valiant men defended Rourke's Drift back in 1879 during the Boer War! The whole Water Point was ancient and had obviously been in use for many years at Archer's Post, continuously pumping thick, hot chocolate.

My problem now was that although I had been sent from the other side of Kenya to provide a 'quick fix' to the problem, I had no access to any spares and realized very quickly that without the necessary replacement parts there was no way of giving the lads out on the ground potable water!

With the help of 3 Para's MT section, we went on a 'recce' of the surrounding area and, thankfully, very quickly discovered an underground natural spring well a mile or two from the camp. The water running into the well was coming from the mountain range many miles away and, after a quick test, I found it to be very pure, perfectly safe, potable water. Our problem was solved! This allowed for a complete rethink of the Water Point and we utilized the Cuplock tower as a large shower unit with S-tanks set up around the tower as mini-jacuzzis, so the lads coming in covered in dust from the field could cool off and relax in style.

Compared to the lads out on the Live-Firing Exercise, providing potable water and running the Water Point was a fairly cushy number. I didn't feel too bad, knowing now that I was providing the lads of 3 Para with the purest water outside of Del Boy's *Peckham Garden Spring*. We also kept the S-tanks filled with freshly filtered and treated water throughout.

On the opposite side of the wide Hot Chocolate River there was, bizarrely, a luxurious five-star safari hotel, very well hidden behind the jungle foliage that grew up from the river's edge. Each evening between 1930 and 2000 hours, I and the 3 Para Assault Pioneer Platoon splashed through the bollock-deep water to cool off below a small waterfall that cascaded down from the hotel grounds.

On the afternoon of our fourth visit, we decided to carry out a stealthy recce of the hotel grounds and would have made the close observation platoon proud that day, by making it through the grounds and into the huge hotel pool unseen. We were even necky enough to order a beer each from a passing poolside waiter!

Soon afterwards, a large group of hotel residents, clad in their finest beachwear, began to fill the swimming pool. After a few minutes, an elderly British gent and his wife swam up to where we were all grouped in the corner of the pool.

"Alright lads, enjoying yourselves?" said the elderly gent.

"Yes marvellous, thanks," we replied.

"I guess you lads are from the British Army camp across the river then?" asked the elderly gent.

"No mate, we're a football team on an East African tour, staying at the hotel for a few days."

Smiling, the gent replied, "Of course you are! Well, enjoy yourselves lads," and with that he and his wife swam off, laughing as they went!

"Fuck! How do they know we are from the camp?" we thought. Looking around at each other, myself in Union Jack shorts and the Para lads wearing identical maroon-coloured shorts, every one of them sporting a set of Para 'wings' tattoos. To cap it all, we all sported that natural squaddie tan when in a hot climate – brown face, neck and lower arms, rest of the body milky white!

We all agreed that our cover had been blown and it was time for us to make a tactical withdrawal. Just as we were about to extract ourselves from the luxury of the pool, another tourist surfaced right in our path and went on to ask us if we had seen the feeding of the crocodiles yet?

"Fucking Mega! No we haven't yet mate. Where do they do that?" We were all looking around, scanning the grounds of the hotel for some walled-in crocodile enclosure, but strangely there was none to be seen. 'Must be around the other side of the hotel,' we thought.

"Just across there, through that gap in the vegetation and at the bottom of the bank rising from the river," the tourist answered, and we all spun round to see the place of his target indication. "Every night at around 2030 hours the hotel staff throw several animal carcasses down the bank to the river, where anything from ten to twenty or more large crocodiles have a right frenzied feed. The hotel staff told us they come from upstream, just around the bend from the small waterfall over there." He pointed towards our nightly cooling-off cascading waterfall platz.

We looked at each other and exclaimed out loud together. "FUCK!" Our bronzed, god-like faces drained instantly to a shade of palest white and, momentarily at least, our suntans no longer gave us away! Our nightly river crossing to the waterfall was the approximate halfway point between a huge crocodile colony and their nightly fucking feeding place!

If you have never believed that Jesus had actually walked on water, as the Bible states, you would have become a sound believer had you witnessed the eight terrified British squaddies that afternoon as we sprinted 'pond-skater like' back across the Hot Chocolate River to the safety of the tented camp. As if the crocodile colony were trying to say "we told you so" the very next morning we found one of them sunbathing a few metres below the Cuplock water tower in a sunken area of the rocks, close to the river!

7. Mediterranean Misadventures

Cyprus, 1995; we had spent the past few weeks at Akamas, living in a tented camp, while we carried out a Battle Area Clearance task around the old targets on the Akamas Peninsular. The targets, twenty-one in total, were a mixture of tanks and armoured fighting vehicles now surrounded by Unexploded Ordnance after years of British Forces attacking them from the sea. Once the surrounding areas were clear, we then destroyed the targets with explosives in order to turn them into manageable sized pieces that could be lifted by the Engineers of 62 Field Squadron, based permanently in Cyprus, who would have carried out the demolition of the targets themselves had it not been for the unexploded ordnance littering the range. Pretty mundane, I hear you say, but I promise you there was also fun to be had...

Akamas and the Saucepan-Lid Spiders

Life in the tented camp was fairly good. We had built our own gym (under the water tower we had constructed); there was a large marquee where we ate our meals and watched videos at night; we were living in two-man tents; we were away from the rest of the Squadron and, more importantly, a long, long way from SHQ!

The only unpleasant aspect to living in the camp was the dreaded trip to the khazi, a small building to the north of the camp, constructed of breezeblocks and housing around five toilets, separated from each other by breezeblock walls. Not only was this small breezeblock building home to five toilets and years of 'spent' British Army compo, it was also home to a family of 'saucepan-lid' sized spiders that had been brought up for years on daily king-sized portions of 'spent' cheese possessed, babies' heads and finest British Army compo chicken curry. They had become viciously territorial and we had our suspicions that, somehow, living on British Army compo and spying on the various troops coming through Akamas over the years, these monsters were now adept at our very own Battle-field Tactics.

On more than one occasion, one of the lads would come charging out of the toilet block, trousers around ankles, screaming like a banshee and hysterically claiming he had just witnessed the saucepan-lid spider platoon executing a perfect left or right flanking attack over one of the walls!

We've Been Expecting You

We had spent the full Sunday washing the Akamas dust, sand and all remnants of plastic explosive from ourselves and our kit in preparation for our planned four-day Mediterranean cruise, taking in both Jerusalem in Israel and Cairo in Egypt. We had actually planned a cruise for twelve of us, but my and another full-screw's passports had been sent back to HQ for renewal and we hadn't received our new ones in time. Not to disappoint, eight of the lads had still gone on the originally planned cruise, two weeks earlier.

Today it was the turn of the remaining four of us – Sgt Bill, Cpl Keswick, myself and Sapper Gordon. We were chuffed to rocks when we tipped up at the port at Limassol and saw our water-borne home for the next four days, the cruise ship *Princess Marissa*, which took up three quarters of the entire port! Looks of relief all round when we realized we hadn't actually been tricked by the Squadron into a four-day 'working experience' on one of our Merchant Navy RFA ships (horrible memories of being on the RFA *Gold Rover* in a Gale Force 10 on our way to South Georgia in the South Atlantic a few years earlier came flooding back – but that's another story to be told in the sequel to this book). We double checked. This ship was definitely white, not the grey of the Merchant Navy, and there was nobody in sight sporting the classic beard and bike grips!

We were having a laugh in the queue to board the ship so allowed all the civvies to go ahead of us, and by the time we reached the boarding check-in we were the last four to board. Our chins dropped and eyes popped out when we were greeted by four stunning young ladies (all dancers from the nightly shows on the ship) and how gobsmacked and chuffed were we when they all smiled in unison and together said, "You must be the four British Army lads. We've been expecting you!"

"Brilliant!" we thought, the eight lads who had gone before us two weeks ago hadn't let us down. Good lads! They had obviously laid the foundations for us. It was going to be an awesome cruise!

The Captain's Table

We had been told by some of the lads from the first trip that the dress code for the evening meals was fairly relaxed and they had received a very warm reception by everyone when they tipped up each evening in Hawaiian-style shirts, shorts and sandals. Well, we didn't want to let the side down so we took their advice, complied with their recommended mode of attire and arrived for our meal outside the restaurant. We gave our room numbers and names to a member of the crew standing at a table outside the restaurant and queued behind the long line of fellow passengers waiting for the doors to open.

It appeared that none of our fellow passengers knew the Dress Code, as they had all tipped up in penguin suits and dickie-bows! Oh, how we chuckled among ourselves. Stupid civvies! If they had ever been in the Armed Services they would know about the seven 'P's (Prior Planning and Preparation Prevents Piss Poor Performance). We all shared the same thoughts, "We'll have to thank the lads when we get back for giving us the heads-up on the relaxed Dress Code, etc. Good lads!"

The restaurant doors opened up and what looked like the restaurant manager came out with two waiters bringing up the rear. The chap who took everyone's names walked up to the manager, whispered in his ear and nodded in our direction. How chuffed and proud were we when he came up, almost bowing, and asked us if we were the four British Army lads from Akamas! When we confirmed this, he asked us to follow him and walked us past everyone in the queue, through the restaurant to a massive oak table at the head of all the other tables. He turned to us and said, "The Captain sends his compliments and hopes you will enjoy the hospitality of The Captain's Table as his esteemed guests." You could have heard a pin drop! The manager then explained that we would have this for the second sitting each night. The Captain and VIPs had the first sitting, but he would be honoured if we were to accept this second sitting and made his apologies that he had not been informed of our stay until it was too late to greet us personally.

We stared at each other in amazement before being ushered into our equally impressive oak seats, and made sure that Sapper Gordon got pride of place on the Captain's Seat. The manager then called on the waiters to allow the other passengers to filter in to the dining room. Needless to say, we received some very weird looks from all the other fancily-clad passengers! It quickly became apparent that we were now part of some kind of weird etiquette. Magnums of champagne appeared, our glasses were filled, and everyone was looking at our table for some kind of guidance before drinking commenced. Sgt Bill kicked Sapper Gordon and told him to make a welcome speech and then to toast the Queen, which he did with much gusto. He received a resounding cheer from our admiring fellow passengers, who were still looking a bit uncertain at the 'Hawaii Five-O' party all grinning back at them from the Captain's Table!

We discovered caviar and lobster thermidor for the first time in our lives that evening, and looks from our fellow passengers appeared to be getting more intent as the evening wore on, especially after we had just finished our sixth bottle of finest champagne. This appeared to be the cue for one of the waiters to open an elaborate box and offer us a 'police truncheon' sized Cuban cigar. I didn't smoke, but there was no way I was going to miss out on any of this unaccustomed luxury, or the pomp and circumstance! We were never likely to experience anything similar again in our lifetimes, so we made the most of it all.

Finally, the manager almost apologetically suggested that we might like to retire to the main entertainment hall to watch the evening's cabaret. He vehemently denied that they wanted us to leave as we were on our third song, and were half way through that British Army classic of choruses, "Jesus Christ, he's so cool, he walks across our swimming pool. Has anybody seen JC?"

We were actually quite grateful as we then made our way to the bar and were able to wash down the rich taste of the caviar and lobster with a few beers. For our remaining three nights at the Captain's Table we surprised the waiters by ordering steak and chips followed by fish and chips, then four large burgers with chips for the final night.

We were entertained by a Shirley Bassey lookalike, a crap magician and the gorgeous dancing troupe, who we quickly sussed as being lesbians (either that, or they were all engaged or married, we decided!). After each dance they would come and sit with us, chat and have a laugh, but we got the strange feeling they were treating us like their brothers! Suffice it to say, no-one even attempted to trap-off with the "Lesbian Dance Troupe" and we just accepted from then on that they had to be gay, as we didn't see any engagement or wedding rings.

That first night we got quietly pissed in our corner. I woke up the next morning in our room and at first thought we were on some desert island. All I could see was jungle everywhere. It didn't take long for my blurred vision to clear and the desert island resolved itself into two enormous ferns in gigantic plant pots, which seemed an odd coincidence, as they were identical to two pots with very similar mini jungles I had seen the night before in the foyer outside the entertainment room, five flight levels above us. How strange!

The King and the Big Yin

After breakfast we went up on deck just as we were docking into the Israeli port of Haifa, 'Gateway to the Near East' (officially opened with the help of thousands of armed British soldiers more than 60 years previously by Lt Gen Sir Arthur Wauchope, the British High Commissioner to Palestine at the time, in case you were interested). We boarded the buses and within minutes the four of us were fast asleep.

I awoke some time later as the bus came to a halt. I looked out of the window. "WTF?" I closed my eyes again, gave them a good rub and looked back out of the window, expecting the 'optical illusion' to have disappeared. It hadn't. I woke the others and told them "You are not going to believe this, but there is a 16ft high statue of Elvis fucking Presley out there!"

Sure enough, we had arrived at our watering stop, half way to Jerusalem at Neve Ilan, 'The Elvis American Diner' FFS! I thought this was supposed to be the Holy Land, not shagging Graceland, Tennessee!

Apparently, Uri Yoeli, a Jerusalem businessman, opened the diner in 1974. The walls are covered with more than a thousand pictures, shelves of memorabilia and souvenirs, including Elvis coffee mugs, postcards and wine that the Yoeli family bottled! He told us that no one in the neighbourhood he was brought up in, or at Jerusalem's only record store, had even heard of Elvis, so Yoeli had to order his first record, a 45 rpm copy of *One Night*, from a shop in Tel Aviv, fifty miles away. To this day, no one ever believes me when I tell the tale of the Elvis Presley American Diner and the 16ft statue in the heart of Israel!

After our Rock 'n' Roll adventure we got back on the bus and headed for the Holy City of Jerusalem. It was at this point that our tour guide stood up at the front of the bus. He was the spitting image of Demis Roussos![7] We believed it might actually

---

[7] Demis Roussos: Greek singer whose career peaked during the late 60s and early 70s. Recognisable by kaftans, a 1:1 girth to height ratio, and the fact that though balding, with a beard, he was apparently still waiting for his balls to drop (you had to hear him!).

have been him when he burst into song and we found ourselves singing along to classics from Neil Diamond's *The Jazz Singer* – I kid you not! When the mini Demis Roussos concert ended, our illustrious guide then turned into Israel's very own version of Billy Connolly. What a character!

In the course of its history, Jerusalem has been destroyed twice, besieged 23 times, attacked 52 times and captured and recaptured 44 times. 'Billy' had a different hilarious story for all of these events.

Jerusalem Japes

We eventually arrived in the Holy City of Jerusalem and entered on foot through the Jaffa Gate and into the maze of the 'souk' (the Old City of Jerusalem Bazaar). We were instantly mobbed by hundreds of Jerusalem merchants, all trying desperately to sell us anything and everything in a street no more than a few feet wide! Genuine Bedouin apparel, saddlebags, rugs, Persian carpets and antiques, as well as modern t-shirts and junk were all thrust in our faces. We felt compelled to buy at least something, so we stopped at a stall selling what looked like genuine Persian carpets. I'd done a bit of haggling in a bazaar in Bahrain a few years previously, so thought that, out of the four of us, I could get the best bargain. To our joy, we were about to find ourselves bartering with Jerusalem's dumbest haggler!

The merchant started the haggling ritual off and asked for $150 for the rug. In true haggling fashion I returned with a "Fuck Off, I could get 10 of these for that price at Axminster Carpets in the UK – I'll give you $20".

Dumbfuck: $120

Me: $25

Dumbfuck: $100

The haggling went on for several minutes until I was hovering around the $40 mark. Dumbfuck was shaking his head and I the same in return. Just as I was about to give in and pay the

$40, he suddenly shouts out "Twenty dollars!" WTF? So I came back with "Five dollars!"

"Deal!" said he. He tied up our Persian rug and thanked us, incessantly smiling away and bowing up and down. The four of us had a good check around for any cameras, just in case we were being filmed for Monty Python's *Life of Brian II* or were to be the stars in a future episode of *Candid Camera* – but there were none to be found. It was confirmed; we had just bartered with Jerusalem's dumbest haggler! 'Nice One', we thought, hardly believing what had just happened, as we headed off to visit the Church of the Holy Sepulchre and the Wailing Wall, which was very impressive. Even more impressive to us were the sandbag bunkers on top of the wall at either end, brimming with an assortment of weapons!

We had just completed our Holy tour when we were confronted with the strangest sight of the day, as we were walking towards the footbridge leading from the Wailing Wall to the Dome of the Rock. We could hear some strange music and someone singing. We stepped onto the footbridge and there in front of us was a geezer dressed up as Jesus, with a halo of thorns on his head and angel wings on his back, sitting on a stool playing a large harp and singing *Waltzing Matilda*! I get the same 'you are talking out of your arse' look whenever I mention the *Waltzing Matilda*, harp-playing angel in Israel to anyone as I do whenever I mention the Elvis American Diner at Neve Illan (for any doubters, the Elvis Presley Statue at Neve Illan can actually be found on Google Earth; unfortunately the Aussie Angel cannot!).

A Camel Train to Giza

It was quite late that night when we arrived back at the *Princess Marissa*. We repeated the previous night's second sitting at the Captain's Table, this time ordering more 'normal' food but managing to drink more champagne, and again finished up in the corner by the bar in the entertainment hall. Once again we were joined by the 'Lesbian Dance Troupe' and another good night was had. After breakfast the next day we arrived in Port Said, Egypt, and very quickly found ourselves on another bus, this time heading for the Ancient City of Cairo to see the Pyramids at Giza and the Sphinx.

It didn't take the four of us long to fall asleep again. This was to be a very long journey, but an undisturbed one, as there was no Egyptian equivalent to the Israeli Billy Connolly/Demis Roussos! Several hours later we were woken up by the bus coming to a standstill and the hustle and bustle of everyone around us preparing to move out. Looking out of the window we guessed correctly that we had reached the ancient city of Cairo on the banks of the River Nile.

Before anyone could get off the bus, however, a large shemagh-covered fat bloke squeezed onto the bus and announced to all the passengers that anyone wishing to trek to the Pyramids at Giza by camel train was to leave the coach here and meet up with it again at the Pyramids. Sgt Bill and I jumped at the chance and before leaving the coach had to pay the Camel man for the trek.

"A bit fucking steep!" we both thought, but then what the heck, we were to head across the Sahara Desert on an epic camel trek; the experience would be well worth the cost.

Cpl Keswick and Sapper Gordon remained on the coach, but we'd meet up later in the day at the Pyramids. So, five minutes later, there we were, perched up high on our 'ships of the desert' wrapped in our newly-acquired shemaghs (bought from the same camel man we paid for our trek) with massive grins on our faces. We each felt like a budding 'Lawrence of Arabia' (LOA) and were looking forward to our epic trek through the Egyptian desert. I hoped the locals had provided plenty of water for the long journey.

Our camel train was a sight to behold, as thirty or forty camels, with an assortment of tourists perched on top, set out. The coach moved out at the same time and we waved enthusiastically to our comrades, who waved jealously back through the rear window of the coach just before it disappeared around the corner of the street. We couldn't believe those two idiots had turned down the chance of a lifetime, of trekking through the Sahara on a camel to reach Giza, home of the Great Pyramid of Khufu (Cheops), the two smaller pyramids of Khafra (Chephren) and Menkaure (Mycerinus) and the mysterious Sphinx! How they would regret it later when we told the story of our epic trek to the lads back in Cyprus, we thought.

Sgt Bill and I were grinning and laughing like idiots as we took happy snaps of each other on our 'ships of the desert' in anticipation of the long journey to Giza through the desert. We hoped we would reach the Pyramids before sunset, so we could take in all the views! We rounded the same street corner the coach had taken just a couple of minutes ago, and...

"FUCK! The robbing bastards!" Rising out of the sand like three enormous pointed breasts, no more than fifty fucking metres away, were the bloody Pyramids at Giza! Our anticipated 'epic trek across the Sahara' ended no more than ten minutes after we set out! We had probably paid the fat fucker on the coach the equivalent of half an Egyptian's average annual income! As if that wasn't bad enough, and to stick the boot in while we were down, when we reached the 'Great Pyramid' our camel guides wanted even more shagging money before they would instruct their camels to lie down so we could get off! Not fucking likely!

The pair of us managed somehow to remove ourselves from the top of these mountainous creatures, each using his own individual method of crashing, sack-of-potato-like back down to earth. Actually, the pair of us admitted to being very glad the journey had lasted only ten minutes and not half the day. It was like sitting on an angry, spitting, growling, eight foot high breeze block. Poor old LOA might have had all that fame and glory and a film or three made about his life in the deserts of Arabia, but he must have suffered from terrible piles after riding around the desert on one of these fuckers for years!

We picked ourselves and our dignity up off the sandy floor, dusted ourselves off and headed towards the small hole in the wall at the foot of the Great Pyramid, where everyone else appeared to be heading.

The Crypt Incident

We reached the entrance to the Great Pyramid and found Kes sat down close by, we were all still a 'tad' hung-over from last night on the ship.

"Where is Ross?" we asked.

"He headed into the Pyramid ahead of everyone else a few minutes ago. I thought I'd wait here for a few minutes to welcome you back from your epic trek," replied Kes, laughing out loud (bastard).

The three of us then walked into the entrance of the Great Pyramid and were gobsmacked when we saw how steep the tunnel down into the depths was (an easy task for three normally fit squaddies, but not so for three still hung-over idiots hardly able to stand). We stared down the tunnel, which was lined every foot or so with a wooden step bolted to the stone floor. Even an experienced window cleaner would have had problems getting down there!

We edged cautiously down 'Jacob's Ladder' into the depths of the Great Pyramid. We had almost reached the bottom when, out of the darkness ahead, we could hear people screaming and shouting. It sounded as if mass panic had gripped our fellow passengers somewhere up ahead. We walked forwards away from the tunnel and into the main vault, brushed past the screaming, panicking civvies to be confronted by a truly horrible scene – a head slowly rising out of the large stone sarcophagus at the end of the vault. We had found Ross! The silly bugger had only gone and crept into the only peaceful place he could find to get his head down for a while – the fucking sarcophagus!

The now hysterical tourists just ahead of us had peeked inside the sarcophagus a minute earlier to be confronted by a body, hands crossed on chest, appearing to be dead to the world. We escorted a rather red-faced Ross past all the traumatized tourists and back up 'Jacob's ladder' for a rest and some fresh air.

We did the touristy bit before leaving Cairo by visiting the mysterious Sphinx and buying the required papyrus paintings from the souvenir shop opposite (mine is still rolled up in its container after twelve years!). The only downside of our visit to the Pyramids and Sphinx at Giza was that I bought the book *Fingerprints of the Gods* in which I unfortunately read that the world ends on 23 December 2012! I made a mental note to visit Egypt again, only sober the next time ... and before December 2012.

Prepare to Repel Boarders – Farewell Egypt

Everyone was rounded up, we boarded the coach and started out on the long, uneventful journey back to Port Said, where the Princess Marissa was waiting for us to board and fuck off back to Cyprus. The massive anchor was 'weighed', the mooring lines cast and we got under way. As the huge ship slowly headed seaward out of the port we walked out onto the main deck, where what appeared to be the entire ship's complement was crowded at the gunwales (nautical term describing the top edge of the side of a boat). Naturally curious, we pushed our way to the front of the crowd and were astonished to see hundreds of small boats and unusual looking floating things that looked more like adapted bath tubs than boats!

Our enthusiastic fellow passengers were throwing all sorts of items down at the hundreds of boats far below. Thinking they were trying to force the horde of small boats away from the ship, the four of us joined in, quickly grabbing anything we could find and proceeded to launch our objects at the boats hoping to score some direct hits and hopefully sink one or two of the little fuckers.

We were in our element when our mad cries of "Prepare to repel borders!" and "Ramming speed!" (accompanied by whoops of joy as we scored a few direct hits) were suddenly the only sounds that could be heard. Our fellow passengers had gone completely quiet and were staring at us with a mixture of horror and disgust.

One of the ship's crew pushed his way through the shocked passengers and came over to us sporting a massive grin as he proceeded to explain to us that it was money and other goods the passengers were carefully throwing to the small boats below, and hauling souvenirs back up on lines of cordage. The boats were full of the poor, needy people from the port area and it had become a tradition for most passenger cruise ships upon their departure!

"So you don't want us to sink any of them then?" we lamely asked. After apologising to our fellow passengers, we very sheepishly moved off the deck and headed towards the bar to lick our wounds and 'splice the mainbrace'.[8]

Barstewards!

Our final night followed much the same pattern as our previous nights on board ship, the Hawaii Five-0 group assembled at the Captain's Table and then regrouped afterwards in our usual corner by the bar, accompanied throughout the evening once again by our friends the 'Lesbian Dance Troupe' (such a pity, as they were all stunners!). We later retired to our bunks below deck and awoke the next morning in time for a last breakfast before standing up on deck watching Cyprus getting larger and larger before we finally docked back in port at Limassol.

Upon our departure from the *Princess Marissa*, all the ship's crew and entertainment staff were at the foot of the gangplank to say their farewells to the passengers. We could see the Lesbian Dance Troupe smiling away at the very end of the ship's compliment line-up. As we got to them and were about to say

---

[8] Originally an order for one of the most difficult emergency repair jobs aboard a ship. On completion of the task, it was customary for the men to be rewarded with an extra ration of rum. Eventually the order 'Splice the Mainbrace' came to mean that the crew would receive an extra ration of rum and became a euphemism for authorized celebratory drinking afterwards. Finally it became the name of an order to grant the crew an extra ration of rum or grog.

our goodbyes, one of them said, "Lads, it's such a shame the four of you are all gay, as we could have had such a fun time together!" We stopped dead in our tracks at the end of the gangplank, staring in disbelief and dismay, first at each other and then at the lovely Lesbian Dance Troupe.

Then the penny dropped! The eight lads, whose four-day cruise I had organized for two weeks earlier, had told all the girls there would be another four soldiers from their unit taking the same cruise. They explained that the reason we were coming separately was that we were all gay and wouldn't have been welcome on the same cruise as the others. They had asked the girls not to mention it to any of us, as it would no doubt ruin our cruise if we knew that word had got out!

You fucking bastards!

But we let them off when we found out why we had been treated like royalty each night in the restaurant and had been allowed to sit at the Captain's Table. The officer who had been on the first cruise two weeks earlier had asked the Captain if he and his subordinates could 'very kindly treat the four soldiers coming on board in two weeks time like VIPs at each evening meal'. He elaborated that we had been granted the cruise at the direct request of the Royal Family as thanks for being part of the team who had acted as personal protection to a certain member of the Royal Family while visiting troops in Northern Ireland a few months earlier. He suggested 'it would not be a good idea to treat the four of them in any way but as VIPs'. Whether the Captain believed the officer or not, they had indeed treated us like kings and had allowed us to get away with wearing our strange attire of Hawaiian shirts, shorts and sandals (even if we did look like four spare pricks) at every evening meal.

8. The Infamous Ball & Chain Awards

For better or worse and for reasons too lengthy to explain here, the squadron emblem for 20 Field Squadron is a kangaroo with a ball and chain attached to one leg. It was a Squadron custom at their happy hours to award a ball and chain to the individual making the biggest idiot of themselves during the preceding week. This was padlocked to the ankle of choice that Friday night, only to be removed just in time for the Monday first parade. Fun? Obviously many people think so, as there are numerous equivalent 'awards' elsewhere, the common theme being 'doofus of the week'. These stories are a small sample from the rich history of the award and its equivalents.

Outboard Motor

I went to Belize in 1981 with 20 Field Squadron and we were introduced to the ball & chain by having the rules explained on arrival. Without going into too much detail, the unlucky 'winner' of the award ended up padlocked to the ball and chain from Friday 'Happy Hour' until Monday morning. A source of amusement on Friday night, the solid steel ball and four feet of chain was no joke when queuing for meals, and was easily capable of causing severe sense of humour failure before it was eventually removed.

We had a section of the Royal Pioneer Corps attached to the Squadron and it was decided that they shouldn't be left out and so were made duly eligible for the coveted title. (Who said "pie 'n' ear?" We'll come on to that.)

I was a good contender for the first week's award as I quickly learned (again!) after total exhaustion, that a Johnson 40 OBM (outboard motor for a boat) will work much better with the spark plugs in!

Not the Sharpest Tool in the Box

Witnessed by my good self and a couple of others was the beautiful sight of a sweat-soaked Pioneer with a bushman's saw in one hand and a small sledge hammer in the other, beating the holy crap out of the saw blade on an anvil with said hammer.

Polite version: "Pray young man, what are you doing?"

Answer: "This saw is feckin' shite and no wonder, the teeth are all over the place, so I'm straightening them."

Just in case 'normal' people are confused by the apparent innocence of that reply, the teeth on a bushman's saw blade are offset, left lean, centre, right lean, very accurately on, sort of, purpose.

The undisputed winner for that week.

The Light of Recognition

The first time I flew south to the Falkland Islands in a Tri-Star, I was sat next to a young bespectacled lad known to all his mates as 'Specky' (you can't beat squaddies for original nicknames!). We'd been in the air for about an hour since taking off from Brize Norton, and he'd been staring out of the window all that time. Suddenly he turned around and said,

"These things don't fly very fast do they?"

To which I replied, "What the fuck are you talking about mate?"

"Well look out there past the end of the wing," he explained, "You can still see the lights from the runway!"

He was pointing at the aircraft's navigation light on the end of the wing!

Suffice it to say, he landed the B&C award in the Sapper Bar at the end of that first week. I was in a troop attached to 20 Field Squadron. Though not a *bona fide* unit member, there was no way I was going to deprive the squadron of this idiot's classic entry to their weekly competition!

Not-so-flash Photography

Old farts like me will remember the days before digital photography when you had to hand your film in at the NAAFI to be processed and pick the prints up about a week later. Well, that's what Pioneer Smith (shall we call him) was doing in the NAAFI queue this particular lunchtime and he was eventually handed his set of prints.

"Been testing my new camera," he merrily declared. Now you or I would probably suss that something was wrong if the first three prints showed the left-hand side of a head and a sunburned ear and would quietly shuffle out of the shop. Not Smithy (shall we still call him). He slowly thumbed through all twenty-four prints of the left side of his head and sunburned ear and stated loudly, "This can't be right!"

"Try turning the camera around the other way next time you use it," came the reply from the NAAFI shop assistant!

"Bugger!" was all Pioneer Smith could manage in reply.

Defective Detection

A mate of mine, who went on to teach at 3 Training Regiment RE, had just been promoted off the square and had taken over the G10 store. He got the Ball & Chain of the week for this corker.

When we got to Kosovo he was tasked to test the Ebex Mine Detectors. First he complained that they weren't working, only to be shown that there weren't any batteries in them, then, when testing them for sensitivity, he complained that they were going crazy, whereupon someone pointed out to him that he was attempting to check them inside a massive steel ISO container!

He's now the Engineer Recce Sgt with the QDG! Hope he doesn't need to check any safe lanes in mined areas for them!

Cold Comfort

I was with 1 Queen's Own Highlanders during Exercise MEDMAN 4 in Canada. The first or second flight out was being booked in at Buller Barracks, Munster when some Royal Engineers rocked up and asked if we could help play a small prank.

Cue HUGE brand new Sapper with small eyes, snout and evidently no brain, formally told by me (as Orderly Room Sergeant) that he had been selected to be Weapons Escort in the aircraft cargo hold.

"Yes, Sarge," was his reply.

We sent them off to Gutersloh and I rang the Medical Centre there who were waiting on the tarmac with an oxygen bottle on a trolley and a medic, who started explaining to said Sapper how to use it and to 'watch you don't get too cold or your willy will drop off with frostbite'.

Meanwhile, CO of the Highlanders, the RE officer and his entire Troop couldn't stop laughing, but still waited until the last possible moment before telling the oxygen-masked Sapper to get his arse on the plane.

Ma Poor Wee Boy

During my first tour of the Falkland Islands in 1991 with 8 Field Squadron, on the swimming pool project, we had a weekly *truth or consequences* session. It was very simple. If anyone was seen dropping a clanger, then when that clanger was announced in the bar you could either own up or take a chance that someone else had also done the idiotic deed and that it was *their* episode that was being reported. Obviously, it was a double bubble, so if you owned up it cost you a crate, but if you kept quiet, ran the risk, and lost, it cost you two.

One of the funniest was when it was announced that although we were well over half way into the tour, one of the blokes hadn't rung his mother. She'd been getting more and more worried about her little boy, so had decided to ring the OC and ask about him.

So who owned up?

After much thought, LCpl B decided it was bound to be him, so he stood up and got a crate in. He was thanked for his honesty and the beer but was told that it was not, in fact, him.

Eventually, after the amount of crates had gone up a few, it turned out to be none other than our much-loved Troop Commander! His name (diplomatically!) escapes me, but he was the same officer who threatened to charge anyone whose webbing fell to bits on a run, only to be handed his own kidney pouches at the end after they had fallen off.

9. Auf Wiedersehen Pet

The BAOR – Postwar Germany, the Cold War, beer and brat-wurst, LOA and tax-free petrol. What were they thinking of? It wasn't entirely voluntary, but thanks should go to Germany and Germans for providing such a long-standing and entertaining playground (at least, you'll believe so reading these little cameos). Pity about the liver damage...

Borderline Brake Failure

There was a section of line on the Iron Curtain where the towers were wood and the fences low and CVRT-mounted cavalry-types would try to put the shits up the Russian border guards by screaming down towards their guard-posts at full whack and then, using the scarily short stopping-distance of said vehicle, bring their Panzer to a halt inches from the tower. Cue white-faced Soviet Bloc conscripts and much hilarity amongst participating and watching wallopers.

On one occasion the Troop Commander decided to join in. His CVRT flew forward towards the tower at Mach 2, got to the braking point ... and the brakes failed, causing the machine to fly straight through the guard tower, which promptly fell over. The CVRT continued (luckily) down the only clear lane in the minefield beyond the tower, finally coming to a halt some considerable distance inside East Germany.

The hapless crew fucked off sharpish and raced back into blue territory. The CVRT was impounded by the Soviets and returned months later, in three lorries, dismantled down to its component parts, all having been thoroughly examined by the opposition.

Spitfire Paddy

In a far-off place and a time long ago, in a Field Ambulance unit high on a hill, a mere eight clicks from the fabled BMH Rinteln, a new bloke was posted in who we'll call Paddy, because he was Irish and because that was his nickname from training. Paddy was rather naïve, for want of a better word, and firmly believed that Alfred Hitchcock's film *The Birds* was soft-porn. One example of this naivety was his reaction to seeing poached eggs for the first time in his life in our cookhouse. Paddy eyed them suspiciously for a while and then asked Scouse M, the AAC cook on duty, what had happened to them.

"Them's poached eggs, them. There's nuttin wrong wid em!" Scouse replied.

Paddy pondered this for a second or two, then said: "Wheel, da next toim yer go out after sum, gizza shout, coz Oi used ta go a poachin wi' me Da regular loik."

Paddy quickly acquired a justifiable reputation for bumbling incompetence and one day received a right royal rollocking from an equally incompetent RSM. The reason he got this rollocking arose because he had been dicked to inspect and repair all the unit's cam nets prior to going out on scheme a week or so later.

Paddy set about this task as only he could, and strung lines high across the length of the stores from side to side, attached to the wooden shelving. This done, his intention was to hang up the cam nets and repair where necessary. Unfortunately, he did it by stringing one line and then immediately draping a cam net over it, then the next and so on. This continued until he had about a dozen nets hanging in the store. However, since he'd started from the window end of the store, the place grew darker and darker with every cam net he hung up.

Eventually the inevitable (for Paddy) mishap occurred. He was on his ninth line or so when, in the self-imposed twilight, he missed his footing on the pile of upended ammo boxes he was using as a ladder and plunged with madly windmilling arms into the nets he'd already hung up. They came crashing down and engulfed him completely. He was trapped like a wild animal in a Tarzan film. No amount of thrashing helped, indeed it only made things worse. If the QM hadn't heard his cries for help as he was locking up for the night, Paddy would almost certainly have been there until the next morning.

Anyway, Paddy thought he hadn't really done anything wrong and that the RSM's rollocking was entirely unwarranted, so he planned his revenge.

There was an official do in the WOs'and Sgts' Mess scheduled for a Saturday evening and the RSM was to attend. At that time, the RSM drove a very flash Triumph Spitfire soft top, which he parked across from the Sgts' Mess in the car park on the evening of the knees-up.

The singlies' block overlooked the car park and Paddy vowed to let all the RSM's tyres down as his revenge. He crept out of the block around 2330 hours into the rain to carry out the deed. We watched from the window as he did the silent SAS number up to the low bushes at the edge of the car park, and then slipped down at the side of the RSM's car. It was actually quite impressive and lent credibility to his pitch about going out poaching with his old man.

So as not to expose himself to view while he was doing the deed, Paddy wriggled underneath the car, reached around the wheel with his trusty matchstick and attacked the valve of the rear tyre nearest to him. He heard a satisfying PSSSS and smiled grimly to himself. Then he discovered that he was trapped and couldn't move, for he'd let down the car onto his own chest.

We waited almost three quarters of an hour for Paddy to return, wondering all the time if we'd somehow missed him slipping back through the bushes. Getting a little worried, I decided to go on a recce and found him, still firmly wedged under the car and thoroughly wet and miserable. Only the gallant action of another six hastily organised comrades, who lifted the car off him, saved him from any further repercussions.

The upshot was that Paddy got to spend ten days in British Military Hospital Rinteln with pneumonia and he also lost the nickname Paddy, which was replaced by "Spitfire". However, he did have the satisfaction of knowing that the RSM, half-pissed, had driven all the way home to the pads patch in Bückeburg and had not only completely trashed his back tyre, but had also managed to grind down the corresponding wheel-rim.

Inflatable Tanks

Soltau Ranges area, around 1975. I drew the short straw and spent far too long as the Troop Commander's driver. He was a chinless wonder, well balanced by being both ignorant and arrogant. He insisted that he got his own way with the civvies, and not being prepared to learn the simplest of German phrases, he merely raised his squeaky voice until they surrendered! Although I spoke fluent German, as far as he was concerned I was sub-human and my job was merely to point the vehicle.

On this occasion he had decided to requisition a barn in a farmyard to conceal three 432s. The approach to the farmyard was a good half a kilometre along freshly-laid block paving, the type often seen in pedestrian zones in German towns. Now three 14-tonne APCs could conceivably damage such a road but 'God' would have none of it. I watched with interest as he and the farmer had an animated conversation, then Troopy walks briskly over to me and snaps, "What's the German word for rubber?"

"*Gummi*, Sir," I replied and he marched back up to the farmer.

Five minutes later he is on the radio calling up the three APCs. Result? A once beautiful driveway now completely destroyed, one German farmer with a now permanent facial tic and heart condition and one hysterical Land Rover pilot!

The true icing on the cake was hearing Troopy explain to the Colonel that the deal had been clinched by assuring the farmer that there were rubber pads on the tracks.

"What *exactly* did you say?" asked the Colonel.

"I said '*Gummi Panzer*'" replied the Troop Commander.

The poor farmer had been under the impression they would be *inflatable* tanks for training purposes. OOOPS!

Getting a Round In

This dates back to the early 50s, a time when the Army was full of Nashies and, with only around 18 months (2 years?) to do in uniform, they just didn't give a toss about anyone or anything. Until the SoFA came into effect we were still an occupying force and could (and did) most anything we pleased. The local CIVPOL had very few powers against us.

The story I heard was about a couple or three tanks on their way to a form-up area. They were making good time and decided to stop at a Gasthaus in the middle of nowhere for a couple of jars before reporting in. The landlord was allegedly ex-SS and let his disdain for Allied troops be known to them. He refused to serve them, so they went back to their Centurions. One of them swivelled a turret, poked the barrel through the big window, loosed off a blank round and they all then continued on their merry way.

Telephones were very few and far between back then so the landlord got on his bike/in his Beetle and went to alarm the local plod. By the time they arrived the tanks were with the main party (and lots of other tanks!) and the landlord wasn't able to identify them. Tango Sierra.

My Other Porch is a Car

A tank commander in Germany on a night convoy was a bit put out when the crew dozed off for a second during a halt. Worried, the commander quickly pulled up to the convoy light of the tank in front. After not moving for a few hours, the commander gave the crew the order to get their heads down. In the morning he opened the hatch to find what he thought was a convoy light was, in fact, the light of an irate German's doorbell.

Camel Capers

Weekend evenings had become a bit repetitive for the lads of 65 Corps Support Squadron in Hameln; same bars, same beers and same discussions, week-in, week-out. On just such an evening a seemingly innocent comment caused ripples of bemused interest as it was dropped into the conversation by one of the more enterprising lancejacks.

"Did you know that the Squadron emblem is a camel?" he asked no-one in particular. The question was largely rhetorical, as every vehicle in the Squadron had a small yellow camel painted on its side, but his next observation sparked rising interest. "And there's a camel in Hameln Zoo, just across the river."

The assembled company immediately recognised his line of thought. A short discussion about the length of time a camel could go between drinks quickly progressed to the more philosophical question of how long it *should* go between drinks and their loyalty to principles of animal welfare soon led to a plan for the evening's activity.

Without the complication of O-Groups, cam cream, camouflage or night vision aids, this small band of MT and Plant Troop stalwarts managed to enter the Zoo undetected, liberate the camel and return with it to the bar where discussion had started. The camel then accompanied them on a pub crawl of their usual haunts.

Too large to pass through medieval sized doorways, it was tethered to the nearest lamp-post and fed its beer there in the street. It seemed to relish the local brew and was soon accused of pushing the pace, usually finishing well ahead of the rest of the group.

The pub crawl continued around the centre of Hameln until the amusement of various passers-by attracted police attention. Undecided whether to charge the squaddies with being drunk in charge of a camel (a mode of transport, after all) but without any local statutes demanding licenses for camels, the police settled for accompanying the party back to Hameln Zoo. The camel was returned to its compound, unsteady but unharmed, the Zoo owner didn't wish to pursue the matter and normal order was restored.

Payback came a few weeks later when the camel fell sick. The only suitable vet was based at the Zoo in Hannover and the camel had to be transported there for treatment. Faced with the problem of loading a large, sick camel into a medium sized horsebox, the Zoo owner obviously needed help. His mind immediately turned to the camel's erstwhile drinking partners and, after a brief phone call, they were 'volunteered' by their Troop Commander.

It turned out to be a hands-on job with a vengeance. The camel sprayed all and sundry with the slurry of its diarrhoea from one end and a bilious green liquid from the other in a spectacular display of projectile vomiting. These emissions were punctuated by loud, noxious farts to the rear and surprisingly accurate spitting from the biting end, but eventually the camel was manhandled into its trailer.

Some clothing was binned rather than contaminate Squadron lines or washing machines. It then took the longest, hottest showers they'd ever suffered to remove the smell, but the first thing down the plughole was any thought that they'd escaped the camel's pub crawl scot-free!

A Moving Experience

A certain Irish regiment was returning to the UK after a tour in Berlin and their Paymaster, who also acted as Families Officer, was confident that he had anticipated most of the likely problems.

He hadn't reckoned on O'Malley.

It was just the first morning at their new barracks following the move when an agitated Mrs O'Malley accosted the Paymaster and told him that she wanted a divorce. He was keen to get both sides of the story, so immediately accompanied her to their new quarter, where she had left O'Malley unpacking their belongings.

Sitting them both down, surrounded by MFO boxes, he thought he'd best get straight to the crux of the problem and asked Mrs O'Malley, "Why, exactly, do you want a divorce?"

"O'Malley's too stupid to be a husband and father!" sobbed Mrs O'Malley. "He's killed the kids' budgie. He left the bird in its cage, covered the cage and packed it in an MFO box for the move."

Not quite believing what he'd heard, the Paymaster asked O'Malley what had possessed him to pack the budgie in an MFO box.

"Well, I thought it would be alright," replied O'Malley. "I put plenty of seed and water in with it!"

A Gulp of Glasnost

Older readers may remember the time when one travel option between BAOR (The Zone) and Berlin was the British military train. It would travel between Braunschweig and Berlin with its doors chained shut, not to keep travellers in but to keep potential defectors out. It would stop at Magdeberg, where the nominated 'Senior Officer' was required to present ID and travel documentation for all personnel aboard. This was taken away, 'checked' by Russian Intelligence officers then returned to the Senior Officer before the train was allowed to continue.

A Sapper friend, then 2IC of the Berlin Field Squadron, often found himself nominated for this duty. He wasn't too impressed with having to travel in Service Dress, but as both male and female representatives were required he was usually happy at the thought of feminine company for the journey. He occasionally complained that the 'femininity' of successive partners was something of a lottery, but he was gentleman enough to admit that if choice of company was a game of chance then his partner was definitely the loser!

He described the procedure at the station as 'semi-formal'. The two officers would march towards their Russian counterparts on the station platform and halt. Each pair would salute, they would hand over the briefcase of documents, salute again and accompany the Russians to their office. They would then sit and wait until the documents were processed, after which the return procedure on the platform mirrored the hand-over. What happened on the platform was carried out in full view of the train passengers, and so stayed formal, but the office wait eventually developed into the 'semi' part of his description.

For his first couple of visits the four officers sat in stony silence. On his third duty the Russian officer's face showed a brief glimmer of recognition as they met on the platform. Half-way through their tedious wait in the office the Russian raised a quizzical eyebrow and motioned to his mouth in the universal invitation to a drink. Pleasantly surprised, my friend smiled and nodded with some enthusiasm. His Iron Curtain counterpart reached into the desk drawer and produced four glasses and a bottle of vodka. Glasses filled, the Russians stood to attention, raised their glasses and shouted "Nazdarovlje!" in unison before knocking back their vodkas. The British reply was less drill-like, as one said "Cheers!" and the other mumbled something about tonic water before they, too, downed their vodkas.

This pattern continued for the next few duties but, apart from the toast, not a word passed between the British and Russian officers. Knowing no Russian, and unable to pronounce the Russian toast, my colleague had used "Cheers", "Bottoms up", "Good health" and was fast exhausting his repertoire of alternatives. Back in Berlin, he explained this brief history to the British Intelligence Corps staff officer and asked, "What's the Russian word he uses for 'Cheers'?"

"Well they usually say *Nazdarovlje,*" came the reply.

"I'm a West Country boy," he explained. "I'll never get my tongue around that!"

"No problem," said his Int Corps friend. "Just say 'Does your arse fit you' very quickly, and he'll assume you're saying *nazdarovlje* with a very bad accent!"

By the time he next travelled, he was determined not to be upstaged and felt fully prepared for the hospitality session. Documents were handed over in the normal way, and they entered the office and sat down. The Russian made the usual gesture, received the usual acceptance and produced the glasses. However, when he reached for the vodka my friend smiled and stopped him with a raised hand. Reaching into the briefcase he pulled out a bottle of single malt whisky and, with a flourish, poured a generous tot into each glass. Standing to attention, he raised his glass and proudly trumpeted "Does your arse fit you?"

The Russian looked a little surprised but smiled, and in perfect Oxford English delivered his first full sentence in almost a dozen meetings:

"Very well, actually. How's yours?"

Caught in mid-swallow, one surprised Sapper Captain sprayed half a mouthful of single malt across the office. The sound of his coughing fit was drowned out by laughter from the other three officers. He recovered enough to smile in reply as he learned that he'd been set up by his Int Corps friend following the request for help.

The Russian officer had spent a number of years in the UK, spoke perfect English and had a wicked sense of humour. He fully appreciated both the joke and the bottle of single malt, which was left with him for appropriate disposal.

Bargain Beer Recce

Three months in a tented camp nestled in the Vulcan Eifel region, just north of the Mosel Valley, promised an agreeable solution to meet 65 Corps Support Squadron's annual military training requirements. The Advance Party of admin staff and instructors set up the camp in best Sapper fashion, including an all-ranks mess (otherwise known as the beer tent).

Local supply was the order of the day, and in addition to fresh rations the cook bought in a small quantity of the local brew to maintain Advance Party lubrication. Initial sampling was expected to be a happy affair, but there were rumblings of discontent over the price of this famous beverage at one

Deutschmark per half-litre bottle. Its slogan was soon being misquoted as "Bitte, ein ... cheaper beer!"

Advance Party elements went about the region on their allocated tasks, but also took on an additional labour of love. An unofficial competition started to find the cheapest beer available. Groups would return from recces and liaison visits with a crate of their most recent find, and tastings were held to determine the best compromise between taste and price for stocking the beer tent. I thought they'd done pretty well when they found a beer and supplier at half the cost of our original choice and for several days this seemed to put an end to competition, but as we all know there's always room for improvement.

Returning late from a trip to the ranges area, I found a small group of instructors huddled around a fast emptying crate in the beer tent. They sounded happy, but looked suspiciously the worse for wear. "You've got to try this, Troopy – it's the ultimate!" came the enthusiastic but defensive greeting. "Competition over – this is less than half the cost of the original stuff *including* the deposit on the crate and bottles. It's the perfect choice for a training camp."

A bottle was thrust into my hand and I downed a couple of thirsty gulps before the reaction set in. It was the worst beer I'd ever tasted. "This is disgusting!" I coughed, "Apart from potential as alcohol aversion therapy, what makes this the perfect choice?"

The reply was delivered with the crafty smile of one about to divulge a deep, dark secret "Well, Troopy, you've only had a quick taste, enough to put most people off drinking more, but the real benefits only kick in after two or three bottles. With this stuff you get the hangover *while you drink it!*"

10. Wuperts and Wodneys and their Wonderful Ways

The Introduction to this book (you did take the trouble to read it, didn't you?) stated "Soldiers are different. Ask any civilian". It should come as no surprise, at least to any squaddie, when I add here "Officers are different. Ask any soldier". A young officer's unbridled enthusiasm can lead to all sorts of embarrassing incidents until it becomes tempered by experience. Unfortunately for many officers, the 'institutionalization' that accompanies prolonged immersion in a military sub-society begins to kick in just as the requisite levels of experience are gained. Only the nature, not the number of amusing stories changes as they 'mature' to successively become crusties, crinklies, and ultimately crumblies before eventually fading away.

Smoking Can Damage Your Health

Maggie Thatcher's visit to the Falklands gave one RE Troop Commander his chance to shine, and he spent the morning running around the site making certain everything was ready. He was driving everyone potty. When the OC asked if everything had been checked, young 'troopy' assured him all was OK. As a laugh, the OC then asked him if he had checked the smoke canisters used to help bring in the helicopter.

You've got it – next minute, smoke everywhere! Well at least he knew they worked. From then on he was known as "Man-Cub" from *The Jungle Book*, as he needed constant supervision.

Stop Horsing Around

Imagine the scene... a cold, crisp winter's day with the sun shining over the Royal Military Academy Sandhurst. The entire

Academy is on final rehearsal for the Sovereign's Parade. The Academy Adjutant prances up on his horse to take the lead, just in front of the Sovereign's Platoon.

At this point, the horse belts out the loudest trumpet of a fart in Christendom, directly in the faces of the finest Sandurst can produce.

Said Academy Adjutant, rather red-faced, turns around and says, "I am terribly sorry about that."

A quick-witted young Orifice Cadet pipes up, "Oh, that's alright sir, we thought it was the horse."

This quip was answered by a pack of Colour Sergeants, Company Sergeant Majors and the Academy Sergeant Major rifting that man to jail amidst great humour of the massed ranks.[9]

Navigationally Challenged

It was a pleasant summer night during the late 1970s, half way through the Standard Military Course at the Royal Military Academy Sandhurst. Most of the basic skills had become second nature by then, and we were enjoying the escape of a night patrol exercise and the relaxation that came with being nominated as "buckshee riflemen" – mere followers for the night. The nominated patrol commander, and hence the officer cadet under the microscope for the evening, was Mr D. Since he was bound for the same regiment as the Platoon DS, whose last CO had been Mr D's father, he was felt to be the Platoon DS's blue-eyed boy. This was soon to change.

Shortly after starting the fourth leg of the planned patrol route, our Platoon DS stormed past (tactically, you understand!) to the head of the column and in a loud forced whisper (not

---

[9] *Editors note:* This could have been included in 'Urban Myths', as the first time I heard the story it was Household Cavalry on a parade during the visit of the Queen of Tonga to the UK. In that version, when the horse farted Her Majesty the Queen apologized to the Queen of Tonga, who gave a similar reply, "I thought it was the horse!" Same story, except that the Queen of Tonga managed to avoid the Guard-room.

entirely tactical) demanded "Mr D! Where the fuck are you going? You're walking in circles!"

Slightly offended, Mr D replied, "No I'm not, Staff. I'm on the fourth leg of the patrol route from the plan I submitted this afternoon."

"Then why aren't you navigating the way you've been taught?" hissed the DS.

"But I am, Staff – I've set my compass, sighted an object on the bearing and we're walking towards that object while pacing the distance for this leg."

Quickly checking Mr D's compass against the patrol plan, our DS came back. "Testicles, Mr D. What object are you walking towards?"

"That cloud, Staff," came the confident reply.

There was stunned silence as Mr D's pointing finger slowly swept an arc across the moonlit sky, following the gentle night wind.

Fool to the Brim

It was early 1979 and 9 Parachute Squadron RE was on its way to Belize. The main body sat in the comparative comfort of an RAF VC-10, happy to have escaped the threat of deployment by Hercules. This meant there would be only one refuelling stop, in the USA, rather than multiple hops via Gander. Most had brought along some source of amusement for the journey, some reading, and many playing cards or small board games to fend off boredom during the long flight.

One young troop commander had decided to show a bit of 'style' on the outward journey. When the announcement came that the aircraft was beginning its descent for the refuelling stop he reached into his in-flight bag and pulled out a Stetson. After managing to fit the whole 10 gallons on his head, he made his way down the aisle with a huge grin on his face, saying "At least one of us has come properly dressed for the airport."

There were barely disguised sniggers from his men, and with a pained expression on his face the Troop Staff Sergeant asked him what exactly he meant. "Well, you know!" he explained. "J R Ewing country, and all that!"

The Troop Staffy put a fatherly arm around his shoulders as he led him gently back to his seat and, pained expression now tempered with sympathy, explained, "It's *Dulles* Airport, Troopy. Not Dallas, Texas – Dulles, Washington."

A Marked Man

Life at Airport Camp in Belize during 1979 was a pleasantly relaxed experience for most, once acclimatisation had made the temperature and humidity bearable. Some looked for additional challenges or opportunities, while others sat back and enjoyed the comparative rest between busy tours. An irksome few, relieved of any significant causes for concern, looked for ever smaller things to worry about; such is human nature. One slightly pompous RAF squadron leader fell into the latter group, and for weeks started most evening conversations with complaints about the laundry service. His reason needs some explanation.

The on-camp laundry was run by Belizean national staff, and consisted of four large, open vats. Washing was done by hand, with clothes being passed through each vat in turn. The first held plain cold water; this removed loose dirt and most plant and animal remnants from jungle patrols. The second contained hot water and detergent, and did most of the cleaning and stain removal. The third was a cold rinse, while the fourth contained starch for those clothes requiring a 'smarter' finish (all items of uniform, RSM's civvies and masochists' underpants). Kit was returned clean and neatly folded, but often came with added 'free gift' characteristics that gave the whingemongers something to grumble about.

The most usual free gift was an unwanted "fourth dunk". Uniforms made up the bulk of laundry, so starching was the 'default setting'. Starched items had to be prised away from the cube of returned clothing, and were more capable of standing unsupported than their owners after a good night out. Putting them on was similar to fighting your way into a new NBC suit; first unhinge along the folds, then peel apart an area of weaker bonding at one of the openings before punching your way into the garment. Fine for uniforms, but not the most comfortable state for your best civilian shirt when starched by mistake!

The second most frequent whinge centred on "bouquet". Water was supplied free of charge to the laundry, so was constantly being renewed in both of the rinse vats. Only clean clothes passed through the starch dip, so that posed little threat to olfactory contentment. The problem stemmed from the contents of the second vat; heating and detergent cost money, so that was refilled only once a day. Clothes washed early in the morning came back with the expected mild post-dhobi fragrance of detergent. As the day wore on, however, the hot soapy water collected more and more of the characteristics of the clothes being washed. By late morning the accumulated essences of a battalion's worth of socks and underclothes festered in this vat and instantly contaminated any clothing that made contact. The concentration was easily strong enough to survive the final rinses.

When returned, these clothes *looked* clean, and were certainly well-pressed, but their scent carried an unmistakeable clue to when they had been washed. A fresh brie; before 0900 hours. Mature cheddar; 0900-1000. Old stilton rind; 1000-1100. Over-ripe gorgonzola; 1100-1200. Anything after that stank like the month-old remains of a sweaty orange-skinned French cheese that their Board of Commerce have threatened legal action over, should it get mentioned by name in this context. Never one to use derogatory terms myself, I nevertheless recognised why others referred to the resident battalion (1 Black Watch) as 'sweaties' – in this case nothing to do with rhyming slang!

No apologies for digression, but enough background information; back to the Squadron Leader. His best civilian Jermyn Street shirts often suffered both these fates, and he complained bitterly. These complaints got stronger with each instance, until he finally bawled out the laundry manager long and hard in front of his employees. A typically laid-back Belizean, the manager was nevertheless a proud man and there was a flush to his cheeks as he quietly promised to give special attention to care of the Squadron Leader's shirts in future. He went on to say that he would personally ensure they were laundry-marked to identify them for individual treatment.

Confident that this intervention had solved his laundry problems, he told fellow mess members that evening how he had put the laundry manager firmly in his place. No-one questioned why he'd brought such good shirts to Belize in the first place, and he ignored their raised eyebrows, shaking heads and smiles as they warned of the possible consequences.

He felt that his confidence had been fully justified when the first batch of shirts was returned. They were beautifully clean, pleasantly fragrant, starch free and immaculately pressed. Blissfully oblivious to the suppressed sniggers that followed him around the mess that evening, it was three days before he realised that his expensive shirts each now displayed a prominent, indelible laundry mark centrally at the back but on the *outside* of the collar.

Luxury in the Field

We did an Exercise in Hohne and the Assistant Adjutant, who was a right babe, came along too. We had reason to visit the HQ and needed to see the ack-adj for something, so we went to her 9x9, knocked on the canvas and were asked in. I couldn't believe my eyes – she'd only gone and kitted the damn thing out with some proper furniture from the Officers' Mess, along with an oil heater, a small but effective chandelier, a painting on the wall, a rug and some flipping 'Regimental Silver'.

Squash and Other Ball Games

US Rangers are on an exchange exercise with British Paras, post US invasion of Panama. Exercise goes well and at the end of the exercise, during the post-exercise piss-up, one of the Yank

Rangers stands up and shouts out loudly "Well, you Brits are pretty tough, but you ain't as tough as a US Ranger."

With that comment, he drops his pants, gets hold of his left testicle in one hand and places it on the table. With the other he produces a hammer and smacks his ball as hard as he can.

"There you go. I bet none of you Brits are hard enough to do that!"

Young troopie, desperate to prove himself to his new platoon duly takes up the challenge... Drops pants, gets bollocks on table and strikes with hammer. Result? He pukes up and passes out.

Turns out the yank had lost a testicle to shrapnel while jumping into Panama and had a plastic cosmetic replacement.

11. The Purple Helmets

The Helmets story is worthy of a book on its own, so we include here just a small sample of the many tales resulting from the antics of its fine members. They should come with a health warning; not for the faint hearted.

Life as a Chocolate Frog (Sprog) in the Armed Forces can be a daunting, sometimes painful and very often, embarrassing, time for the unfortunate newcomer, but for any Chocolate Frog unlucky enough to have been posted into 58 Field Squadron (EOD), Royal Engineers (specialists in High Risk Search) in the late 80s it can only be described as their worst nightmare come true! The Purple Helmets was a somewhat bizarre organisation forced to go underground for many years due to its 'dark side' and basically not being very 'liked' by anyone in authority, or by any grown up within the Regiment lacking a sense of humour. A brief history of their formation and a few stories relating to them are outlined here. Throughout this story and most of the stories in the book names have been cunningly replaced by 'Letters' to protect the innocent and the not so innocent.

The Origins of the Order

The Helmet – the symbol of the Order – was discovered at Kineton whilst the lads were on a Battle Area Clearance task. After a disastrous day, masters H & G retired for an evening in the closest bar – the Pioneers'. Whilst Sapper H distracted the 'guppy-like' barman with tales of EOD adventure, CPL G snuck in behind the bar, swiped the Helmet and made off down the corridor. On arrival back at Lodge Hill the Helmet was given its distinct Purple colour – for obvious reasons – and an Order was born.

The BDO

From there, CPL G's enthusiasm called for all future Helmets to undergo some form of initiation ceremony. There were many different ceremonies to terrify new Helmets over the years, but the one experienced by most was the BDO – not the Steely-Eyed shortened version of "Bomb Disposal Officer" in this case but the dreaded "Bedford-Drop-Off", a mutation of an earlier ceremony based around a Land Rover.

This ridiculous ceremony involved dropping from the tailgate of a Bedford truck – travelling at 40 miles per hour across a ploughed field. Forbidden to protect himself, the candidate was expected to drop (according to Helmet SOP's) 'sack-of-potatoes-like' onto the rushing field below.

The results were as to be expected: cartwheeling, whirling, broken-fingered sappers, battered by stones and large potatoes, strewn about the Kent countryside like bodies from a plane crash.

Trunk and Disorderly

Assigned an Oldsmobile and driver by the U.S government, the Helmets cruised around the town of Tucson – eight of them in the car and one, Sapper W, in the trunk. As they drove round the town, listening to the Sex Pistols and getting drunk, their memories of W in the trunk faded. After an hour or two, they arrived at their final destination, The Cactus Moon nightclub, where, without a second's thought, they piled out in search of young women and a light ale.

As the Helmets square-danced the evening away and the women swooned – naturally after an hour or two, Ws confinement in the trunk became too much. In complete darkness and without a single clue where he was, he began to bang on the trunk and shout out to passers-by.

"What the fuck's going on? Are you lot out there?"

For the people passing in the car park it was like discovering the unfortunate victim of a Mafia kidnapping. Standing around the car, bent low, with their ears close to the trunk, the bewildered pedestrians asked if he had been abducted and if he was injured.

As the scene worsened and the decision to call the Police was debated, more and more people gathered around the talking trunk.

Confused by W's garbled, English accent, shouting, "Look, just go and find me the fucking Helmets! They'll be in there somewhere..." the Americans stared at each other in amazement.

"The Helmets, gee... this guy must be real fucked up!"

At this, W started to get annoyed and more than a little concerned.

"Listen, for fuck's sake... Go and get me the Purple Helmet Display Team and tell them to bring the fucking keys! How many groups of British squaddies do you have in there anyway?"

And with that, the penny dropped and one of the bouncers went inside to address the PA system.

"I'm looking for the Purple Helmets, are they out there? There's a man in the trunk and he would like to get out."

Hearing this, half the dance floor froze, looked round at each other and simultaneously mouthed the words, "Sapper W – Fuck!" and then burst into laughter.

Sapper W was eventually freed and, to the amazement of the gathering crowd, showed no concern other than regret for the ale he had been unable to quaff during his incarceration.

After the States came a couple more jobs, the trip to Gibraltar, and with it the worst decision in a long time – to walk, after a serious night out on the tiles, to the top of the 'rock'. Helmets, hampered and abused by spitting monkeys, struggled upward on a needless pilgrimage to the top.

Gibraltar behind them, the Helmets returned once again to 'a small town in Scotland.' With the completion of Perth, and the Troops' stomachs full of deep-fried mars bars and pizzas, the bedraggled Order packed away their collection of soiled ladies undergarments and made their way back home, bringing to a close the single, longest and most eventful piss-up in Helmet history.

The Harrop Rocket

Spending more time than usual in camp, misguided Helmet energy was channelled into drinking binges at the 'George' and 'Doddy', destructive and slapper-unfriendly parties in the lines, and the great firework fiasco. Prior to the troops' departure from an exercise at Thetford, an entire town's worth of fireworks was purchased and transported to their 'hide location' in the lines (accommodation) at Chattenden. (Such a good time was had trying to skewer each other with rockets on exercise, that it was considered an excellent idea to bring back the goods and continue our escapades within the camp.)

All began well, with the firework Range confined to the accommodation alone, the Order escaped the scrutiny of camp authority.

On many occasions, upon returning from the George, H's moped was wheeled out and a candidate – usually an unfortunate, sober 'bayonet frog' – was dragged from his bed and placed upon the seat of doom. His mission was to pilot the 'Harrop Rocket' along the Helmets' corridor, a corridor filled with the choking smog of CS gas and slippery with spilt beer and bodily waste.

Outfitted with gas masks and armed with rockets and air-bomb repeaters, the Helmets waited in the doorways of rooms as the Sprog, protected only with H's human cannonball motorcycle helmet, began his suicide run.

When you consider the close quarters of the accommodation and the size of target, it's not surprising that impacts were often and accidents common.

Coitus Interruptus

Sprogs weren't the only people to receive 'character building experiences.' One female visitor was to be subjected to more hair-raising tricks than anyone in the Squadron.

'Slurp', as she was affectionately known, was to be put through some horrific trials during her stays within the lines, the most memorable of which involved CS Gas, a few rolls of Harry black masking tape and an open window.

While bouncing up and down on top of one of the troop members, she was oblivious to the giggling group that had assembled outside the Sapper's bunk. A large juicy orange had been placed on a small table next to the bed. Unbeknown to the mating couple, the said orange had an Outdoor Sound Unit (these are like small training detonators that are usually only meant for training outside and pack quite a punch, especially when contained as in the orange!) inserted into the middle of it. Command wires were camouflaged on their journey out of the slightly open window and down to a Shrike exploder.

On the word of command from above, the Sapper in charge of the Shrike primed then fired the Shrike. The sound unit detonated and the said orange 'blew up', covering the passionate couple from head to toe in wet, juicy, sticky orange juice, absolutely perfect for the next phase of the attack! Utilising the 'spoon method,' they then crushed a CS gas pellet, set it alight and began to blow the fumes under the door and into the room.

For those who are not familiar with the effects of CS gas, without going into a lecture, it basically burns the skin, causes choking and irritates the eyes with the same intensity as concentrated shampoo or Deep Heat. Worse still are any areas that are covered in sweat. With the pores open, the particles have easier access and are absorbed swiftly.

As you can imagine, Slurp, after half an hour of 'bedroom fun' was dripping with sweat. Her 'lovefest' went from ecstasy to agony in about 30 seconds. Eyes streaming, and sweaty body in absolute torture, she could only watch, horrified, as her caring partner reached under his bed, donned his respirator, blew out hard, shouting the words "Gas! Gas! Gas!" then leapt off the bed for his dressing gown. In severe pain and totally confused, Slurp tried the door, only to find that the sneaky team had 'harry-blacked' it up, leaving no way for her escape.

Signalling to her through the choking smoke, her thoughtful partner, clad in his protective bathrobe and gas mask, steered her toward the open window.

To Slurp it must have seemed the only escape, but the bunk was two floors up and too far to leap. Settling for anything to alleviate the pain, she jumped onto the windowsill and, still naked with her 'fun bags a wobbling,' stuck as much of her orange soaked, stinging body out as possible to the cold night air.

Giggling from the adjoining bunks, the Helmets, in an act of mercy, threw cold water and captured the moment on camera.

However much amusement was to be found in the corridors and the confinements of the lines, it wasn't long before the Helmets, tired of young, defenceless targets, moved their attention elsewhere.

The Battle of the Burger Van

The first firework attack was initiated by 49 Field Squadron (EOD). Their target was the burger van, which parked on the regimental Drill Square every Wednesday night to provide sustenance to unfortunate Sappers leaving the 'Stomp' with Chatham Growlers. The subject of an omni-directional rocket attack, the van's unfortunate occupants could do nothing to protect themselves but batten-down the hatches and pray that the guard arrived before they were suffocated by hot dog steam and burning burger fumes.

Recognising a golden opportunity, the Helmets took over the fight, and the games commenced. Nightly attacks on the guard were commonplace and, as a possible deterrent, dog handlers were re-tasked from anti-terrorist patrols to lurking around the darkened corners of the camp in the hope of grabbing a 'Firework Bomber.'

Wise to the new countermeasures, the Order employed timer devices, utilising improvised cigarette fuses to gain the upper hand. Accommodation searches were another futile tactic employed by the authorities to reveal the phantom menace –

but to no avail. Of course, the weapons were never discovered – a Search Troop gathers many skills in the course of its duties, one of which is the ability to hide things cleverly.

For all its good times and well-meant adventures, events went from amusing to serious in very little time. Challenging the Army system, the nocturnal rocket attacks went on when they should have stopped. Eventually, with the Squadron threatened by spending Xmas in trenches in the local woods, the operations relaxed and all was quiet again. Although escaping serious disciplinary action, the antics of the Helmets were not to go entirely unpunished. The Squadron was lined up and warned by the CO, "If the capers of these Purple Headed Warriors don't come to an end soon, there'll be big trouble." A clear message had been sent to the Squadron management: I don't want to hear of this group again.

The Helmets were forced to go 'Underground'

The Mekong Guard Shift

In the early 90s, being the Regimental lepers suited the Helmets down to the ground, serving only to strengthen their resolve and widen the divide between themselves and authority figures. In the wake of the Firework Drama, in the opinion of the senior figures, the Helmets had transformed from a permissible group into a threat, to be forbidden a free rein and tolerated no longer. With the understanding that the lads would receive little or no support should they 'drop a bollock' and come to the attention of the local Police Force, piss-ups were held in secret and T-shirts worn when the group was away on tour or at a special occasion.

A memorable example of the underground Helmets was the Mekong Guard Shift – members B, M, G & W. Shaven-headed and without eyebrows, following a 6-month eyebrow-shaving campaign, the four large, skinhead gargoyles that lurked the main gate in early '92 were to terrify many a civilian truck driver unfortunate enough to visit the camp at that time. It was quite a scene: the Commanding Officer, gawking through the side windows of his Vauxhall Cavalier as he received a salute from his now hairless purple-headed warriors.

The year saw several new arrivals, many in tune with the Order, but some, usually the individuals from training centres, who were not. The majority of sprogs at that time were a different breed. Entertained by computer games and other fandangled gadgets, they didn't share the Helmets enthusiasm for walloping slappers, shaving eyebrows, CS gassing each other and booby trapping each other's possessions with various non-lethal explosive devices. It was not uncommon whilst walking back from dinner, or emerging from the toilets, to see a group of giggling Helmets unravelling electric cable away from a sprog's bed space. With the deft touch of the command wire upon a live battery, an almighty bang would echo down the corridor and another victim of an improvised claymore device, filled with last night's curry and pummelled Helmet faeces, had just received his first 'character building' experience.

12. All-In Stew

Having written or collected much of the material for this book, we thought it helpful to gather stories with a common theme under a single chapter. Not as simple a task as one might think, encumbered by the Jonathan Smiles' schizophrenic tendencies. Willing to shuffle and deal between proposed chapter subjects, we nevertheless found that there were always some stories left over. These are they...

The Kit Kat and the Old Lady

My most embarrassing moment was after a bit of live firing at Otterburn and because I'd picked up an injury I ended up brass sorting with the Platoon Sergeant. Everyone had gone back to camp by the time we finished so we headed home in the rover. We'd been going about an hour when he started to nod off at the wheel, so he pulled into a service station. He stayed outside to get some air and I went in for a brew and a KitKat. It was quite late and I was the only person in there until a little old woman came in. She bought a cup of tea and two fairy cakes and sat opposite me.

After polishing off one of her fairy cakes she then proceeded to take a stick of my Kit Kat and munch on it greedily! 'Cheeky bint,' I thought, and swiftly grabbed and swallowed one of the remaining three sticks myself, before the old bag could get her chocolate-coated paws on it, at which point she gave me a look like a summons and, quick as lightning, grabbed and chomped down the last two sticks of my chuffing KitKat!

As she was a little old dear, I couldn't really go off on one, but thought 'I'm buggered if you are getting away with it'. I stood up to leave, picked up her other fairy cake, went right up to her face and with a 'MURRUMPPHH' sound, stuffed her cake in my mouth in one and walked out, feeling quite satisfied.

We got back in the rover and continued on our way. About fifteen minutes into the second leg of our journey I fancied a ciggie ... and when I put my hand into my pocket I found **MY** KitKat!

Time Off for Bad Behaviour

As a brand new Sapper troop commander, I was wary about potential scams and jokes awaiting the 'new guy'. Nevertheless, I was all innocence when one of my section 2ICs approached me immediately after a morning parade, and, in full earshot of his section, asked:

"Troopy, I need to take Friday afternoon off. My wife is having a baby."

It was only Monday morning so, worried there might be some complications, I innocently asked, "When is the baby actually due?"

His reply was quick, and sparked off a riot of laughter from the section.

"Well, if you give me Friday afternoon off, Troopy, about nine months time!"

Cover Story

Young Brian seemed destined to be one of life's victims. He was more naive than the average five-year-old, without the five-year-old's ability to erect tents or assemble flat-pack furniture. Also clumsy and uncoordinated, the only time he found himself the centre of attention was after the crash, splash or crunching sound he'd just caused. If he'd been a Sapper, then demolition would have been his forte (if he ever got over his timing problems!). In short, he was a walking disaster, but one of the most good-natured guys you'd ever wish to meet. I think we all know a 'Brian'.

Given his lack of coordination, it wasn't easy to put Brian and ball-games together in the same thought. It took someone with more imagination than I had to realise that there might be a use for his destructive gifts, and to try him out as tight-head prop for the Squadron rugby team. His efforts on the field met with mixed success, but he was soon a valued social member of the squad.

Doubly qualified, as both squaddies and rugby players, it goes without saying that the post-match social scene featured beer in copious quantities. This made it a fertile research environment for people-watchers studying the variety of drinkers' urination habits. Some, camel-like, never seemed to take a leak; others would happily last four or five pints, then blast the porcelain with a high-pressure stream worthy of a carthorse (two paces left/right close march for those either side!). Most, myself included, would easily last out the first three pints, but once the first leak was taken, the pattern for the rest of the evening was one piss per pint.

Despite these different patterns of relief, there seemed to be one common factor. It was a reflex action amongst players, as is widespread throughout the military, to down their drinks before taking a leak. Not Brian. He seemed to have a direct link between bladder and legs, bypassing both brain and common sense, and would leg it for the bog the second his bladder cried "Full!" This carelessness soon endeared him to the near-skint members of the squad, as he would usually return to a circle of smiles, innocent whistling and an empty glass.

It was quite some time before he developed any 'minesweeping' counter-measures. On an evening like any other post-match piss-up, Brian was quieter than usual and sat smiling to himself as he picked at the back of a beer mat. When the time came for his first slash, the usual suspects had edged closer to his table. His glass was still three-quarters full. With all the signs of his usual urgency, he rose to his feet for the hurried march to the gents, but this time paused briefly to cover his pint glass with the beer mat he'd been picking at.

Overcome by curiosity, as well as the pull of an unattended pint, the vultures swooped to his table to find that he'd scrawled a message on the picked, white surface of the beer mat: "I spat in this pint. Signed, Brian"

Bladder relaxed, Brian sauntered confidently back to his table with a smile on his face; he could see from across the room that his pint was still three quarters full, and that the beer mat still covered the glass. That smile lasted all the way to the table, but his face fell when he got within reading distance. It was definitely the same beer mat, as he could read his own inscription, "I spat in this pint. Signed, Brian." What wiped the smile off was the addition underneath.

"So did we!" followed by seven other signatures.

Back to the drawing board!

Public Inconvenience

A young troop commander returned home to Newcastle on his first leave following successive courses and met up with a group of old school friends for a mini reunion. They had all gone their separate ways after leaving school, so conversation was as varied and interesting as the drinks they put away during their city centre pub-crawl. Last Orders came around all too soon, but just in time to preserve consciousness, and the customary post-pub curry went down really well. Conspicuous consumption led to conspicuous behaviour, and they were eventually asked to leave the restaurant.

After eating and drinking so much, the need for intestinal relief was inevitable, but for our troop commander it came sooner and more urgently than expected. No way would he be allowed back into the restaurant, and a sprint to the nearest public convenience just revealed that in Newcastle city centre at that time they were locked at 2300 hours each night.

As they staggered along in search of a solution, desperation was beginning to turn to panic when one of his friends spotted an unlit blind alley and offered to stand guard at the entrance while Troopy made his deposit. Pained expression on his face and paper hankies at the ready, he rushed to the far end of the alley, dropped his trousers and leant back, bracing himself against the wall. Pent-up pressure made sphincter relaxation swift, and a little less than voluntary. A huge sigh of relief escaped from one end as he relaxed into full flow from the other.

There was absolutely nothing he could do as the double doors of a fire escape opened up directly in front of him and the bemused cinema crowd filed past on their way home after the late show.

Aim for the Poop Deck

Back in the day when I was Operations Officer on an Exercise, we'd had a particularly rancid weekend with a couple of NODUF incidents that left me behind a desk dotting 'i's and crossing 't's. I hadn't realized how late it was until the RSM came in and told me that the transport boys, as he put it, 'couldn't find their nuts in their pants', and the last troop transport had already gone, leaving us without a way back, especially since the Adjutant and CO had 'booked off early' with the command car.

The RSM was a former Sergeant with the Duke of Edinburgh's Royal Regiment in the UK, who had taken early retirement and moved to the Colonies, but after three weeks in Civvy Street had decided to 're-up'. Many of the small brass hated him because he would always comment on their plans and assignments by starting off with, "Well, in the *Real* Army we did it this way..." but, I loved the old git. He'd been in Cyprus just before me and we often traded stories over where the best beaches and letching spots on the island were.

After a bit of phoning around we found out that the CO was still on base, waiting for his other half, who was coming to get him in his brand new minivan. Thankfully, he offered us a ride back, as there was plenty of room in the vehicle.

The 'other half' eventually arrived in the shiny new car. It still had some of the showroom plastic on knobs and such. We proceeded to throw our rain-soaked, mud-covered post-exercise kit into the back and climbed in. The CO took the command chair and I got to ride shotgun, Mrs CO riding in the second tier with little one-year-old CO Junior strapped into a baby seat behind 'Daddy CO', leaving the RSM with the back seat all to himself.

We were motoring along quite nicely when I detected a strong aroma of decaying flesh mixed with flayed skunk in a Chinese food shop wheelie bin! The CO's nose was twitching, too, and he began to make throat-clearing noises.

Mrs CO smiled weakly and said, "Oh, dear... I think junior has made a doo-doo." I looked back and the kid was grinning ear to ear and the RSM was digging frantically in his bergen for his S10 Respirator. There was no lay-by or rest stop in sight, and besides, the CO didn't want to delay further, so the matter fell to Mrs CO to do something.

All women are expert at handling bodily fluids that would make the average grown man blanch. Unhooking the gas master, she balanced him on her knees, whipped off the clothes, pulled off the cack-filled disposable diaper and wiped, powdered and re-kitted the tyke in record time. Even the RSM was impressed. I think he was timing her and comparing the exercise to field stripping a GPMG.

Well the 'wee un' was back to normal, but the offending effluent, though now tightly wrapped up, was still stinking up the van and rolling down the windows just moved the stench around. Trying not to gag, the RSM said, "Allow me to dispose of that for you ma'am." With one hand, he grabbed the little bundle while with the other he opened the sun roof and, with a precision that comes from years of grenade practice, lobbed the stench-ball in a perfect arc out of the van.

Mrs CO and I watched in fascination and even the CO kept a keen eye on the trajectory in the rear view mirror as it soared up and then came down to land on the front seat of a boat being towed in the opposite direction, exploding on impact and splattering the windshield of the fast-receding sportscraft!

The rest of the ride was spent in silence.

The Mamores and the Ring (Piece) of Steall

It was the morning after a night bashered up next to the river opposite the Youth Hostel in Glen Nevis. Unfortunately, our hapless four (for the story to be known as W, X, Y and yes, you've guessed it, Z) discovered they had strung their bashers up at the heart of the Midgie Clan Gathering of 1996 and were covered from head to foot in midgie bites. They wearily headed off through Glen Nevis to carry out their mission for the day, which was to get up onto the Mamores and complete the trek around the "Ring of Steall".

After an eventful crossing of the steel rope bridge, where all four decided to cross at the same time and see how bouncy they could make the crossing, the small group finally made it up on to the Mamores in record time. They decided to rest on the summit of An Gearanach, the first Munro of the day, at 982 metres, and make a brew and a 'boil in the bag' each for lunch.

The going is fairly easy once you are up on the circular ridge of the Mamores and it is just a case of keeping to the well-worn narrow path up and down each Munroe along the way. For the first hour or so our party of four was being met by people walking in the opposite direction who smiled friendly, warm greetings. 'These strawberry mivvies aren't all bad,' thought our hapless band, and greeted each one in a similar friendly, warm manner. From about an hour or so into the walk, the friendly greetings began to thin out very fast! Much to the confusion of the hapless group, the 'friendly forces' coming in the opposition direction began to get very unfriendly looking, and passed by with what looked like looks of disgust on their faces – bleedin' civvies are all the same after all!

It wasn't until the group finally stopped for a rest from their epic yomp along the Mamores Ridge, pausing on one of the final Munroes, that they discovered the cause of the sudden change in manner of all the civvies they had passed over the past hour or more. There, standing up while the other three had collapsed to the ground getting ready for another brew, up was young Sapper Z, who had been bringing up the rear for the entire duration of the Ridge Walk, wearing nothing but a massive grin on his face, his walking boots and the day sack on his back! Stood there in the bollocky buff he happily declared, "You can't beat this naked Munroe walking can you?"

He went on to pass the All Arms Commando Course a year or so later, where he would, no doubt, have been able to continue his Naked Trekking.

To cap off an eventful day, the gang of four, who by the end of their trek around the Mamores were totally knackered and in need of rapid cooling, decided to strip naked and charge as one into an ice cold crag pool. The stampede didn't stop until they were in the middle and deepest part of the pool, where all four suddenly cramped up in pain at the same time, all going underwater and being unable to help each other due to laughing so much. It was a miracle all four made it back to the edge of the pool, much to the amusement of a party of German tourists, who had stopped to fill their water bottles and take a rest in serene surroundings but instead were confronted by four soaking-wet, naked, laughing idiots, rolling around on the floor in agony!

None of us will forget the day we walked the Mamores 'Ring of Steall' – with our last man giving every strawberry mivvie who passed a view of his own 'Rusty Ring Piece'.

Happy Days!

Free Slices of Bacon Please

I was in the works canteen this morning. My usual SOP is to wander in, buy two pieces of toast and wander back out again. All the breakfast stuff is a buffet-style affair. You grab whatever you want and give some money to the one-toothed hag behind the till.

This morning was different. I walked in. No-one behind the till. No white toast. I stuck my head behind the kitchen door and said to the lard-arse who makes the food, "Any chance of some white toast, please mate?" The reply seemed helpful enough: "No probs, it'll be out in a minute."

I went back out and waited by the empty toast plate. I had a bit of a look round. Still no-one at the till. Lovely! I grabbed two pieces of bacon and quickly stuffed them in my grid. I'm not bacon's biggest fan, but stolen bacon has a taste all its own. As I started chewing it, the till-dragon came back from smoking her Kensington Javelin (99p for 500) and clocked me. Trying to look innocent, I turned my back to her and carried on troughing my pilfered treat.

When the toast came out, I'd managed to swallow the bacon, so was able to pay for my two pieces of warm bread (42p, the robbing twats) and not the bacon (30p a slice you fucking thieving Arabs!). Job well done, I'd say.

Being the introspective sort of individual that I am, I took to thinking about my thieving. Why did I nick the bacon? I had the dosh and I don't even like bacon that much. I came to the conclusion that, like blimping and bezzering, pilfering is a skill best kept well-honed.

The Wedding Wrecker

Weddings are always great for mixing civvies with squaddies, with universally disastrous results...

One of my mates from Aldershot had somehow persuaded a girl that didn't look like Jocky Wilson in a wig to marry him. She truly was a few steps up from the usual fare and when all her family turned up at the church it was apparent that they had a few bob and were not overly impressed with their daughter's choice of husband. Pity they didn't get to choose the best man either.

He picked a complete 'heed-the-ball from the line shack' to do the honours. We were all on the standard squaddies' table at the reception (the one nearest the exit door, between the bogs and the kitchen, at the furthest possible point from the bride). When our man got up to do his best man's speech, he sent off the first warning signal to her family by shouting, at parade ground volume, "You lot on the back table, keep the fucking noise down!"

As he started his speech they were already looking alarmed. He put his hand on his wife's shoulder and said: "Before I launch into my speech, I've got a small announcement to make. Helen has told me to expect to start washing a few nappies..."

"Aaaah," they all said, "Perhaps he isn't horrible after all."

He continued, "... Apparently all the muscles in her arse have packed up."

I found it funny, as did my ten mates, but of the hundred and forty there, a hundred and thirty weren't laughing, the miserable cnuts.

He finished off with what is, to this date, the most inappropriate wedding anecdote I've ever heard.

"I'm having a lovely day, so I'll finish with this little story (mass groan). Everyone in the block knows that Pete's got smelly feet, but last year it got ridiculous. The smell was killing us. After a week of threats we couldn't get him to change his socks, so had to take drastic action. We moved all his bed space in the drying room and made him live there. He lost 40lbs in three days, but blow me down, the smell didn't go away. Turned out it wasn't Pete after all ... Someone had had a shit in one of the empty lockers and it had gone off."

The Bingo Caller

'Say it clear, say it loud, I was a Squaddie and I am Proud.'

One of the structural surveying firms we use took us all out for a meal on Friday night. Best behaviour was observed all evening. Right from the first beer in the Sawyers Arms and throughout a lovely dining experience at Café Istanbul, including expensive wines and swanky kebabs, I played a blinder. My mum would have been proud. The large lady seated next to me at the meal was the wife of one of the surveyors and I spent the evening being utterly charming to her. I laughed at all of her rubbish jokes, smiled at pictures of her kids and didn't take the hump when she kept beating me to the banquet dishes.

Anyway, I took the time taxi at about 12:30am when we'd moved on to a bar to get properly shite-faced and woke up at

06:00am on my sofa. The rest of the weekend was spent pleasantly reminiscing about an evening well spent.

I got into work that morning and was met by another ex-squaddie, who simply said, whilst chuckling and shaking his head, "What are you fucking like?"

As the colour drained from my face, he filled me in.

This larger-than-life lady had been wearing a sleeveless dress. She was busting out of it all over and it was apparent that she'd needed a banding machine to get the bugger on. According to my mate, I walked up behind her while she was taking a drink, grabbed hold of the skin hanging beneath her upper arms, shouted to him, "Check out the fucking bingo wings on this one!" and proceeded to waggle them about from left to right, so that she spilt her drink. For some reason, this upset her and she stormed off to tell her husband.

Me being the world's worst fighter, it was fortunate that he looked like Arthur Askey's little brother. Apparently, he gave me a severe ticking off while I stood there, boss-eyed and grinning like Jack Nicholson. My only defence was to plead, "Come on, they do dangle down a bit, don't they?"

And the moral of the story? If you're fat, wear a jumper.

"I'll be right back lads..."

During follow-on Combat Engineer training after basic, at 3 Training Regiment in 1986, one of my room buddies, Andy Deacon had just gone through one of the permanent RP Guard Commander Corporal Ted Otter's (God rest his gentle soul, the bastard!) forty-minute beasting sessions in the guardroom at Gibraltar Barracks. I found him collapsed and gasping for air, halfway up the stairs on his way back to our room after his 'session'. He didn't want to go to the med centre for fear of incurring the further wrath of Corporal Otter, so we placed him on his pit, moistened his lips with water and loosened his clothing. We stayed in the room for fully half an hour before we went to dinner, in case he was in danger of going downhill.

Later that evening we were all doing our 'Combat Engineer Best Books' when Andy, now bright as a button and merrily going about his Admin, but mysteriously not doing his Best Book this night, said that he would do the traditional nightly NAAFI run (usually the first to finish their daily update of their Best Book would volunteer for this).

Everyone wrote down what they wanted in the notebook he produced and he then collected our money and went off to the NAAFI... but he never made it back to the room with our feast that night. Instead, he opted to jump the camp's perimeter fence and went AWOL!

Roll forward seventeen to Basrah in 2003... I had served in the EOD Regiment for my final few years in the Army and since getting out had worked extensively in the Mine Clearance/Explosive Ordnance Disposal field with several different companies. At the time I was working for an American company as an advisor for the mines/UXO clearance for the reconstruction of Iraq. Almost to a man we were former 33 Engineer Regiment in our previous military lives and had already been into the main part of the Airfield and introduced ourselves to the RE EOD lads who had been in the conflict and were now happily coming to the end of their tour. We had invited the Boss and his EOD lads around to our tent situated opposite 53 Field Squadron RE's abode on Basrah Airfield. We managed to 'acquire' a couple of crates of real alcoholic beer from our Jordanian camp master (not the gay variety but the 'in charge of our tented quarters' sort) before the EOD party appeared at the tent. Our invited guests arrived and we all sat in a big circle and real beer was handed out to all and sundry. Stories aplenty were then told, and many a tale of derring-do was recited by this valiant group of steely-eyed chaps.

After a good 30 minutes of getting to know our newly-acquainted friends, I couldn't help but wonder where had I seen the skinny, bright red faced, bald RE Signals Staffy before... and then like a blast from the past it hit me. Earlier I had been introduced to this guy as 'Andy Deacon'

"Andy Deacon? Andy BLOODY Deacon!" I thought. Recognition dawned. Now I couldn't help but stare and all sorts of nasty, revenge-filled thoughts entered my mind, but alas! I realised I had matured over the years and had also changed in size and appearance since this underfed, ravaged and over-beasted wretch of a civvy was being slowly but surely turned into a trained soldier all those years ago (17 to be precise!). He didn't recognise me and my own twisted thoughts of torturing him over a large fire in the sand dwindled as the beer flowed.

With bitter thoughts now completely gone from my mind I thought at the very least I would remind him of his past, and couldn't help myself when I said out loud: "So fellers, just how much interest should one get on 10 Great British Pounds over 17 years?"

Everyone stopped talking immediately, all staring at me as if I had completely lost the plot. All, that is, except one now even redder, but still as bald RE Signals Staff Sergeant who had dropped his can of 'real beer' as recognition finally dawned on him. He was now staring in absolute horror, eyes on stalks, chin on tent floor, at the former Squaddie who sat opposite him sporting the biggest grin in the history of really large grins.

"And where the fuck is my bottle of coke, family-sized bag of cheese & onion Walkers crisps, three Mars Bars, two Snickers and my chicken & mushroom Pot Noodle, you thieving, fence jumping twat?"

Fucking Priceless!

All was forgiven over the next few beers, especially when a still red-faced RE Sigs Staffy returned the 10 Great British Pounds quietly at the end of the night after 17 years. I declined the offer of another 10 pounds to cover the interest; the laugh we had was more than enough to compensate. We learned that he had gone AWOL that fateful night back in '86 as he was in fear that he wouldn't survive another beasting at the hands of Ted Otter, so opted to go on the run instead. He gave himself up a year later and this time completed his training.

Trust Me – I'm a Pilot

The Army Staff College trained selected officers for higher things. Many of those selected had until then only limited experience of other arms and services, so courses included a series of demonstrations to help fill gaps in knowledge and understanding. The Corps all regarded these as very high-profile events, since they were an opportunity to shape perception in the minds of future generals. Each of the Corps organisers therefore felt it vital, even as we worked towards a digitised battlefield, that their demonstrations ran like clockwork. It was difficult to imagine a better way to tempt fate, or a more opportune set of circumstances for Murphy's Law (if it *can* go wrong, it *will* go wrong) to be observed.

The Royal Engineers' Demonstration of 1989 was to be the last of its kind, future productions having been cancelled as one of many economy measures. Rehearsals were numerous and thorough, but because of the number of agencies involved, the elements came together for the first time only at the final rehearsal. Attendance at the actual event was limited, but there was a lot of wider interest, so to take full benefit of the showcase there was also full attendance at the final rehearsal, at which the audience included enough high-powered attendees to make it just as high-profile as the actual event.

Against this background, it came as some surprise when the Wing Commander responsible for the RAF supporting elements stated that the aircraft would only appear for the demonstration proper. He maintained that these were, after all, 'the most professional pilots in the world and fully capable of getting it right first time.' However, as a former Sapper, the Brigadier's experience was based more firmly in reality and he insisted that the RAF elements appear for both the Staff College Demonstration and its final rehearsal.

History was to prove him right.

The demonstration took place at Hawley Training Area, nestled between Camberley, Farnborough, Cove and Fleet on the Surrey-Hampshire border. A large spectator stand was erected, overlooking a natural amphitheatre surrounded by woods, where the first half of the demonstration was to be presented. Guests then moved to nearby Hawley Lake for second half. There were four RAF contributions to the programme, split between these two sites and planned as follows.

The first was a spectacular attention-grabber. A Harrier, moving fast, used the dead ground beyond the amphitheatre to approach unseen and unheard. It then suddenly appeared, as if from nowhere, and made a strafing run as twin lines of battle simulation charges replicated ground strikes across the bowl of the amphitheatre, directly towards the spectator stands. The combination of surprise, realism and volume of sound was calculated to wake up anyone within half a mile and focus spectators on the rest of the demonstration. It was enough to get some running for cover!

The next two RAF elements were both simple culminations to specialist phases. At the end of the Harrier Support demonstration a Harrier started up in its hide, taxied to its pad, took off vertically in front of the spectators, then transitioned to level flight and flew off. Following the Armoured Engineer presentation a Chinook flew in, hooked up to one of the equipment bridges laid on the area and transported it away underslung.

Not a lot to go wrong, one might think...

The final contribution took part at the lake and was an insertion of RE divers by Puma. The helicopter simply made a low-level pass, dropping divers into the water to carry out a simulated reconnaissance for ferry operation. The lake was shallow in parts so for safety, and to keep the action centre- stage for spectators, the drop had to be made within a large rectangle designated by marker buoys; another "bread and butter" task.

That, in four nutshells, is what was *planned* to happen. What *actually* happened at the final rehearsal made the whole event far more memorable and must have convinced the Wing Commander that Murphy (of Law fame) was out to get him.

The weather seemed a good omen, as the day of the final rehearsal dawned clear and bright. Preparations all went to plan, perfected during the many dry runs that had included every 'P' imaginable (speak to any instructor for explanation of at least seven). Spectators took their seats in the stand and the buzz of conversation died away as their attention turned expectantly to the start of the demonstration. There was a sudden collective intake of breath as the roar of a low-level Harrier assaulted their ears and, with perfect timing, the ground before them erupted in a staccato series of explosions that rapidly traced twin lines of 'strikes' directly towards the spectators.

The three seconds of silence that followed could have been shock effect, but puzzlement and confusion were more likely causes because, although timing had been perfect, some spectators never saw the Harrier. Instead of targeting the amphitheatre, the pilot had lined up on the only other open area in that part of the training area, a disused airstrip about 200m to the north. Strike one!

Normal service was resumed and all went well until the second Harrier's spot. Start-up and taxiing went as planned, and the aircraft rose vertically from its pad. Then, instead of the expected dip of the nose and gentle transition to level flight, the Harrier pointed its nose at the sky and its engine roared full-on as the pilot attempted a "rocket man" departure (there's probably an RAF term for this manoeuvre, but I'm not sure it would convey the same combination of 'flash' and 'Hollywood').

It may have been the amount of throttle required, or more probably the fact that this was attempted too close to the ground, but the end result was less than impressive. The downward blast of jet efflux raised an enormous cloud of dust and debris which enveloped the aircraft. Suddenly ingesting more solid matter than was healthy, the change in the engine note was barely perceptible but the Harrier began a backward, downward slide. The pilot did well to recover just in time for a violently heavy landing less that 20m from a trench full of Sappers, accompanied by some very expensive sounds (from the aircraft, not the Sappers). Strike two!

Less to go wrong with the Chinook bridge-lift, one might think, though many have voiced reservations about an aircraft capable of having a mid-flight collision with itself. Everything seemed to be going to plan, as the mighty beast beat its way into the arena and hovered above the bridge. It was quickly hooked up and the lifting strops quivered taught as the Chinook took the strain. Then ... nothing. A dynamic demonstration suddenly became a still-life study, but for the turning rotors. Try though it might, it could not raise the load and eventually the bridge was jettisoned without having left the ground. The Chinook disappeared into the distance, tail metaphorically between its legs. It turned out that the pilot had left nearby RAF Odiham with a full load of fuel, leaving insufficient lift capability to handle the bridge. Strike three!

As any follower of American Rounders will tell you, 'three strikes and you're out', so the RAF didn't feature again until the second innings down at Hawley Lake. It may have been a misguided attempt to impress and make amends; it may have been pilot exuberance; it could have been a simple miscalculation. Whatever the reason, instead of a steady pass at the appropriate speed and drop-height, the Puma shot across the lake and attempted to slow to a safe speed only at the last moment. As the downwash was directed forward to achieve this rapid deceleration, the loadmaster's view was totally obliterated by the cloud of spray that enveloped the aircraft. Unable to see the marker buoys, he couldn't dispatch the divers. The planned smooth pass would have demonstrated a semi-covert insertion, with the helicopter in view for no more than 10-12 seconds and little sign that divers had been dropped. Instead it screamed in, disappeared in a cloud of spray, dithered in the general area of the drop-zone, rose to improve visibility then sank to drop the divers before scooting away. Batting average maintained.

It's probably just as well that RAF radio traffic wasn't too closely monitored that day. Suffice it to say that the Wing Commander was quick to personally apologise to the Brigadier and that RAF professionalism was displayed to better effect when all went superbly on the actual demonstration.

So next time you need to call for Close Air Support ...

13. Military 'Urban Myths'

A number of stories reappear periodically in different guises, or told in a different setting. Sometimes this is the mark of the raconteur's skill, massaging the facts to appeal to a particular audience, but sometimes the stories have more to do with imagination than memory. By describing these as 'urban myths,' we acknowledge that the grain of truth may be small and difficult, or impossible to find. We would do no more than quote a particularly gifted raconteur, who would maintain, "never let the truth get in the way of a good story!"

Rapid Response

A squadron of Scimitars from the Blues and Royals were on exercise at Otterburn Training Area in early 1982. It had all just kicked off big style in the South Atlantic and the OC (or Squadron Leader or whatever these donkey-wallopers call them) was told to get his boys down to Southampton (Marchwood) sharpish. He decided not to wait for the tank transporters and briefed the boys for a Squadron road move.

Once everything was sorted, the OC jumped into his Volvo Estate and buggered off down the road, only to be overtaken at 70mph on the M1 by a troop of his Scimitars, receiving an immaculate 'eyes left' from each of the commanders as they passed him!

That Sinking Feeling

A well-known west country Armoured Regiment on KAPE decided to ferry the Mayor of Dartmouth across the Dart in the back of a Stalwart, together with CO and part of the band playing sea-shanties or some such.

Unfortunately, it seems the vehicle had been on public display in Torquay the day before and nobody noticed that somebody had made off with the bungs. At least, nobody noticed until they were halfway across the river, by which time it was too late. BLOOP!

The Name Game

RSM to UOTC Officer Cadet: What's your name?

OCdt: Paul, Sir!

RSM: PAUL??!! I'm not your fucking mother, I'm the Regimental fucking Sergeant Major! Now, I'll ask you again – what's your name?

OCdt: Officer Cadet Paul, Sir!

RSM: *(pause, two-three)* Now, don't I look a fucking cnut?

OCdt: (Barely conceals grin, but wisely keeps quiet!)

Beam Me Up Scotty!

The scene is some parade somewhere, long ago. We were all standing there in our ginger marching suits being inspected when the inspecting officer comes across one guy with a lump in his breast pocket and the pocket undone.

Cue much shouting and jumping up and down. Said soldier calmly reaches into the open pocket, pulls out a packet of smokes, flips the top open, holds it to his mouth and says, "For fuck's sake beam me up Scotty, it's shite down here."

Pause for breath... "GET AWAY! Left-right-left-right-left-right-left..."

Just a Thought

New Recruit on parade, says to Drill Sgt: "Sir, Can I be jailed for thinking something"

Drill Sergeant: "No, of course not! Unfortunately"

"Well Sir, I think you're a cnut"

"Lef', Righ', Lef', Righ'" – Straight to Jail Do Not Pass Go!

Gas Precautions

Before the very first Exercise UHLAN EAGLE in 1996, the Battle Group Commander was having a meeting with the Polish commander of the training area. On asking about training restrictions he was told, "Do not use nerve gas within three kilometres of any inhabited areas."

Just Like Flying a Kite!

A few years ago WRAF recruits were taken up in a Dakota or Hastings aircraft for an hour's air experience flight. One pilot introduced himself to them on the ground, took off, then got two balls of string and attached each of them to the Co-pilot. He then backed out of the cockpit, unrolling the string, not forgetting to stop halfway down the aisle to make some 'steering adjustments'.

He then got two young WRAF recruits to stand up, gave them the balls of string, told them he needed to take a leak, and asked could they just keep the plane flying steady.

Needless to say, when he got to the back, he was straight on the blower to the co-pilot, who started banking the aircraft while those two girls tried to steady it, amid screams and growing panic.

A Familiar Culprit

During Op TELIC, at the end of the tour, one of the Locally Employed Civilians (LEC) who ran a shop came up to the RSM complaining that one of his soldiers had an outstanding debt of about £3,000.

"It won't be a problem as I know his name!" says the LEC.

"Go on then," says the RSM, "What's his name?"

"Harry Skinters," came the unlucky reply.

Mistaken Identity

While stationed at Woolwich, one of the lads in our troop had been out on the town and had a few beers and went to get a replen from the Lloyds 'hole in the wall'. He took out his wallet and his card, put his wallet on the cash point and inserted his card, but the hole in the wall immediately closed down. Just to really make his night, it also had a glass screen which came down, totally encasing the whole machine with his wallet on the inside.

As he carried out emergency retrieval techniques with his size 9s and a traffic cone, a police car pulled up and nicked him. The police were very understanding when he explained what had happened and when they stopped laughing they called out the standby bank cash point filler.

Turned out he had put his ID card in by mistake!

Guess My Name

This actually happened to me! Asked by the Company Sergeant Major what my name was, I promptly answered. The CSM then screamed "Are you taking the urine? This isn't an 'effin' game show!"

My surname? 'Guess'!

Second to None

My uncle, who served in Korea, was driving past a huge US Military Logistics base and read a sign which said something like "101st US Army Quartermaster Corps Base Operations facility – SECOND TO NONE."

He drove on for a couple of hundred yards in the pissing rain and turned round a bend in the road where he saw two British Sappers under a sheet of wriggly tin (corrugated iron sheeting) making a brew. Nailed to the tree beside them was a simple chalk sign, which read "NONE".

Pick Up a Penguin

What about the RAF bloke employed at RAF Stanley to stand up the penguins after they fell over watching helicopters fly overhead? Could very well be true![10]

Language Barrier

Training Depot/Regiment ... room inspection, first day...
    Troop Sergeant: You comfy here son?
    Recruit (Scot): No Sergeant, I come fae Glasgie.

Crazy Horse

There was, according to legend, an infamous RSM who went by the nickname of "Crazy Horse" who reputedly jailed:
1.   His wife – for walking over the square.
2.   A coke machine – for taking his money and not giving him coke.
3.   A table – for collapsing while he was standing on it giving a drill demo.
4.   His pace stick – for falling over on parade.
5.   The Guard – after (see 4, above) pace stick was marched off the square under escort and placed in a cell. The guard had removed said pace stick from the cell to wash the floor. CH then jailed the entire guard for letting a prisoner escape.

Sounds like an entertaining chap!

Easy Rider

There is a story about a Cavalryman who used to go around the barracks on a pretend motorbike, mimicking the sitting position and making all the broom-broom noises. In an establishment where you were expected to march smartly everywhere, this was soon noticed. The trooper was evaluated and

---

[10] What about the penguins at RAF Stanley who would peck up the Crabs after they fell over leaving their Happy Hours?

it was decided he was unaware of his actions and not deliberately trying to be MD'd so he was discharged.

On his way out of the barracks, dressed in civvies, he was stopped by the Provost Corporal of Horse.

"Not going home on your motorbike lad?"

"No mate," the now ex-trooper replied. "I've left it outside the block for the next bloke who wants out of this shithole!"

Paper Chase

He was as normal a Sapper as you could find ... with one exception. If he saw a piece of paper lying around he would dash off, retrieve it, scrutinise it, then drop it, muttering "That's not it!" before carrying on as if this was normal behaviour. The lads obviously noticed this but after the standard verbal battering had died down, they left him to his weird little ways.

However, one day he was spotted by an officer who, with concerns for the chap's mental state, brought it to the attention of the Unit Medical Officer. The MO informed the CO, who ordered the poor bugger in for a wee chat with the MO.

The Sapper eventually went in front of the CO, who explained that according to the MO's report he was physically fit and healthy but was mentally unstable and therefore would be medically discharged.

The CO then signed the discharge paperwork, at which point the Sapper dashed forward, picked up the paper, read it, and with a smile spreading across his face declared, "That's the one I've been looking for!"

Adding Insult to Injury

We had a guy in my old Squadron who was a bit thick, to put it mildly. One day he was cleaning the winch on an 8 tonner and was holding onto the end of it when being wound back in. Either he didn't realise what was about to happen or else wasn't paying attention. Result: his left hand was drawn into the guide rollers and he lost a couple of fingers.

Typical squaddie sympathy followed. The QM storeman billed him for the glove that was trashed, we crated him for being unable to order ten beers by holding up his fingers and he also had to get the beers in for short touring!

Hapless Heroes

During the firemens' strike a Green Goddess and its squaddie crew were dispatched to assist an old lady whose cat was stuck up a tree. Quickly reunited with her precious pet, the old lady offered the crew tea and biscuits. Glad of a break from the tedium of standby, and keen to bask in some positive PR, they accepted.

It was all smiles and goodwill until they waved their good-byes. Pulling away, still smiling and waving, they ran over the cat they'd just rescued, killing it stone dead.

The cat's name was 'Lucky'.

I've since met three Sapper troop commanders who all claim to be the culprits.

14. Negligent Discharges

The stories in this chapter do not refer to a medical condition or probable cause for female disappointment, but don't judge prematurely! They may be just as painful, and are often more embarrassing. But enough of my banging on; the examples that follow will ensure that understanding comes quickly.

The wisest of soldiers will tell you, "Never fire a single round ... that's definitely an ND! If you fire many, then you obviously saw something."

Not 'North Dakota', 'Notre Dame' or even 'Doctor of Naturopathic Medicine', and most definitely not the academic qualification of Republic of Ireland fame, the 'National Diploma'; Pull Up a Sandbag's ND is the military one – "Negligent Discharge" described by the dictionary as 'an accidental/involuntary discharge of a firearm involving culpable carelessness'.

It is more often described by the average squaddie, however, as "The Military Cardinal Sin of all Military Cardinal Sins, almost always carried out by the Unit Fuckwit, who has been visited by the Emperor Mong (See chapter on Emperor Mong for more detail) or alternatively as a 'Bang-Fuck' (if you've made it prematurely go bang, the natural reaction is to shout "FUCK!") If said ND happens, as it very often does, whilst 'clearing' said weapon into an unloading bay, claims from the culprit of being a 'One Metre Sniper' must always be ignored! Not surprisingly, ND stories told by any squaddie or former squaddie are always about the storyteller's mate or 'someone they knew'. Strange, but true.

Here are a few of the very best NDs as carried out by real soldiers (not the dipping in the boiled egg variety):

Calamity in Kuwait

Doha Harbour, Kuwait City early March, 1991. We were a Combat Engineer section that had set up the desalination water supply point for the British 1st Infantry Division (4th & 7th Armoured Brigades) moving north from the city as soon as it had fallen to the Allied Forces.

At Doha the Royal Engineer EOD lads had swept through the buildings and the harbour area for booby traps and were clearing the compound a few hundred metres away by the time we moved in. Although there were no obvious booby traps, a large Ammo Dump's worth of weapons and ammunition were scattered throughout the harbour – like *Toys 'R' Us* in terms of fun to be had for the average British soldier!

After a few days making safe anything obvious and marking off anything dodgy-looking for the boys from Bomb Disposal to have a closer check later on, the only 'toys' that were left for us to play with were various weapons, ammunition and shed-loads of grenades, which we enthusiastically 'disposed of' with much firing of all manner of foreign weapons, and fishing with grenades later. Our final remaining 'toy' was the biggest of all, none other than a huge Patrol Boat, reputedly the Kuwaiti Navy's only surviving vessel of any description – 'Kuwait Navy Patrol Boat P402B'.

Naturally, curiosity got the better of us all, and we soon found out that by pulling on one of those funny-looking levers next to an even funnier-looking large white pod-shaped contraption, an inflatable lifeboat was instantly launched that inflated to the size and shape of the Millennium Dome. Within minutes we had nigh-on filled the harbour with three identical bright red and orange floating monsters. We had to leave one of the pods unfired, as we had run out of room! Each Dome contained a rather Gucci Japanese all-singing, all-dancing survival kit and the carrier holdall for all this survival malarkey was equally impressive.

We were on our way off the boat, laden with our new-found and very impressive-looking 'sports bags', when one of the lads mentioned we hadn't had a look at the 'Four-Barrelled Anti-Aircraft Gun' that was bolted on the main deck towards the bow of the boat. The weapon was pointing out to sea but we decided not to mess around with it because since our arrival a couple of days earlier there had been a constant stream of American Chinook helicopters going back and forth across the water in the direction the weapon was pointing. Besides, we knew very little about the weapon and it was clearly loaded, so we decided to give it a miss and leave it to the EOD lads to take a look at and make safe at a later date.

Later that afternoon, our Staffy and young Troop Commander came up from the Milk Factory in Kuwait City to see how our section was faring and to bring us a welcome supply replen. We sat in a circle, munching our newly-delivered 'fresh' rations, sharing a few mugs of tea with the troop management and recounting the story of our first few days at the Doha harbour. Naturally, when the stories of copious quantities of weapons, ammunition and hastily-dumped equipment were told, we included an account of the Patrol Boat and the lifeboats we had 'discovered' floating in the harbour! At that point, one of the lads scurried away and brought his newly-acquired 'Survival Sports Bag' into the circle to show our troop management. Troopy's face lit up when he spied the goodies inside the bag and he asked us if there were any more. Without thinking too hard, we mentioned the unfired pod on the boat and that there may well be one more of these floating 'Domes' inside the pod.

Troopy stood up and raced over to the Patrol Boat after getting a hasty target indication from us. We didn't think any more about it, as we were too busy enjoying our fresh rations and drinking good old mugs of tea...

Then, all of a sudden, all hell broke loose! We thought we were under attack as hundreds of large calibre rounds broke the silence what seemed like inches above our heads! Mugs of tea and fresh rations went flying everywhere as we all dived for our weapons and for cover! No more than 30 seconds after it had begun, the firing abruptly stopped. A head count was called out and just as we started to emerge from our various cover positions, a very red-faced and shocked young Troop Commander appeared.

"You Fucking Cnuts! Why didn't someone warn me the left and right foot pedals on that Four-Barreled Gun on the front of the boat don't turn the weapon left and right but are the BLOODY Firing Mechanisms!"

We looked at each other in total bemusement before bursting out laughing. Our young Troopy had found out the hard way how to fire the weapon (something one of us had been very close to discovering earlier but thought unwise to mess with!). He had wanted to spin the thing around, but when he stepped on one of the pedals and the weapon starting firing, the shock of this had momentarily glued him in his position. As he had no idea what he had done to cause the weapon to start firing, he had sat there with his foot firmly pressing down the pedal for almost 30 seconds before realizing! We, and especially our young Troopy, were lucky to get away with the events of that day, especially as upon seeing Troopy wandering back into our location we could hear the faint *wokka-wokka-wokka* of a Chinook in the distance.

We named that one the TCAT–FOND (the Troop Commander All Time – Fuck Off of Negligent Discharges). That was a secret never to be told, well at least not until the publishing of *Pull Up a Sandbag*! Sorry, Sir, if you are reading this (you know who you are!) but at the same time, it was fucking hilarious – afterwards!

Unseen Enemy

A mate of mine, on his Junior Brecon, is on stag with a GPMG and somehow manages to let one off without trying. As quickly as possible, he carries on blatting away with the GPMG and when the DS come over to find out what all the shooting is about he calmly points out the 'enemy' at the edge of some forestry block 200yds away.

Of course, no enemy were there, but instead of a charge and getting RTU'd from Junior Brecon for the negligent discharge of the first round, he just gets called a 'blind fucker' by the DS for thinking he saw enemy in the forestry block and taking appropriate action.

Missile Misfire

One of the more expensive NDs took place in the Falkland Islands in 1982. One of the Air Defence Batteries' Rapier surface-to-air missile launchers went tits-up and the Techies were called out to fix it.

All appeared to go well as the Techie went through all his tests and found nothing untoward with the system.

The Techie then tells the Rapier Operator to press the fire button, just to test the system when – WHOOOOSSSHHHH!!! a Rapier surface-to-air missile leaves the launch platform at Mach 2.5! He had forgotten to disconnect the firing lines!

The launched missile luckily didn't hit anything and eventually crashed into the ground more than five kilometres away and started an underground fire that burned for two months!

Not Quite Bang on Time

We were firing a ceremonial salute for some noteworthy event with 105mm, a battery of six M2A2s (blanks only, fortunately) and it was my first time actually firing the beast. The Number One says, "When you hear the command, give the firing toggle a good tug."

The time comes, the BSM gives the command, I pull the toggle, and all I can hear is a loud bang from the battery.

After the smoke clears the Number One says, in a slightly worried voice, "I don't think it went off," to which I reply, "I'm sure it did – look, I'll prove it." Pulling the toggle again, harder this time – BAAANNNNGGG!!! "Fuck!" says I.

Being the centre of attention is lovely, but not in the middle of a parade. It's pretty hard to ignore the large bang and cloud of smoke coming from the muzzle of a 105.

Oh how we all laughed... NOT!

The Ultimate ND?

Of course there is the Ultimate ND. A Phantom Fighter Jet pottering around Germany in 1982, spots a Jaguar Jet returning to its base. As is the wont of the fast jet jockeys, he decides he's going to 'get a kill' on the unsuspecting Jaguar.

He makes his approach, sets himself up, gets the lock on the lead, presses the tit and thinks "Oh shite..." as a heat seeking missile whistles merrily on its way, seeking out the heat of the Jaguar's engine! He tries to warn the Jaguar but has no clue what frequency he's on.

From the Jaguar's point of view, they are flying back from a training sortie, feeling all warm and fuzzy and heading back to their base at RAF Bruggen in time for a well-earned glass of sherry, a fine selection from the mess cheeseboard and a few select vol-au-vents stuffed with prawns in an Italian aurora sauce, when they suddenly hear an almighty bang!

All the warning lights on the panel come on, including 'engine fire' and the sound of the engines disappears. Said Jaguar pilot hears his No 2 on the radio telling him he's on fire. Since everything seems to have gone 'Pete Tong', he makes the only sensible decision remaining and ejects to safety, thus sealing the fate of his rather expensive kite. [ii]

Result? Surely the biggest ND in the history of the ND!

A Negligent Declaration

A lady of my acquaintance was a middle-ranking civil servant at the MOD. One day she attended an air show with a lot of VIPs.

[ii] The Phantoms had been on a battle flight scramble practice out of RAF Wildenrath and were doing some practice intercepts. The crew of the Phantom forgot that they were carrying live weapons, so when they pressed the firing switch they thought they would just get the growl needed for the simulated missile launch so they could film the attack. Instead they fired a live Sidewinder Aim-9G missile, cutting the rear of the Jaguar in half.

During the show a fighter aircraft turned turtle and the pilot ejected – safe and sound fortunately.

That evening as my friend mingled among the great and the good at a very posh champagne reception to promote the arms trade she chanced upon the Chief of The Air Staff. He asked if she had enjoyed the show.

"Oh yes" she said, "I particularly enjoyed the bit where the pilot ejaculated."

15. The Emperor Mong

We can all recall scenes in cartoons or older films depicting a struggle of conscience. You know the form; angel on one shoulder advocating 'the right thing', while a small devil on the other tempts the subject with wicked suggestions that sound far more interesting! Now, to many it appears that squaddies are far more decisive than their civilian counterparts, and the reason is simple; there's nothing angelic about a squaddie! However, a squaddie's temptations aren't confined to the wicked or evil variety. They include a high proportion of 'easy way out' options that appear far too innocent to interest the average devil, and furthermore need more subtle presentation if they are to succeed. On the squaddie's shoulder sits no mere devil, but a lord of twisted logic, the undisputed ruler of the realm of temptation... Behold, the Emperor Mong!

Emperor Mong 'shorts'

Cyprus, Exercise LION SUN 1988. A landing craft stops 30 metres from beach and the ramp goes down. The exalted Emperor Mong whispers in the Troop Staff Sergeant's ear, "These RLC chaps must know what they are doing, so it won't be more than a foot deep." The order is shouted for all to debus. Chaos prevails a moment later as the entire troop debus into 3 metres of water!

My No.1 EM has to be the time I went on a five-day expedition with no gas for my cooker. He told me there would be loads of places to buy it (there weren't, so I ate cold compo).

It is three o'clock in the morning and you have just come off stag. It is snowing and you are freezing and knackered. You get into your gonk bag and try to zip it up, but it gets stuck half way. You know you should try to free the zip, but a voice in your head says, "You don't need to do up the zip! You will be quite warm enough. Just go to sleep!" This is the Emperor Mong speaking, the most mischievous being in the universe. Twenty minutes after you go to sleep you will wake, freezing cold and won't get any sleep for the rest of the night.

"It's only a 24-hour Op – you don't need waterproofs."

"You'll see something you recognise on the map soon, just press on..."

"We're nowhere near the border..."

On a freezing cold day, with my gas canister all but empty, I hit upon a Great Idea. Physics; Combined Gas Law, right? A small volume of gas with low pressure... I can *encourage the flame* a bit by heating the canister. My mucker is a devotee of hexamine and his stove is burning merrily... I can tell you're ahead of me... as was he as we dived in to the shell scrape. Luckily, his dive knocked his stove over and my canister rolled away from the flame before natural selection could run its course. The Emperor struck big-time that day!

"Relax, your mate will never find out, besides, she's gagging for it!"

 "My son, it's only *this far* on a map..." [pinches fingers together] The cnut didn't say it was 1:1,000,000 scale map – of another country.

"There'll be plenty of time to sort your admin out later. Have another pint..."

"You will not need to top up with diesel. It's not that far and supplies are bound to be available when you get there."

"Of course it's the right connector. What makes you think there could be any other type?"

"Four thousand charge bags? In one big pile? No problem." How we laughed all the way to the burns unit!

"Don't worry, being a bit gobby with one's elders and betters in the mess on a Friday due to too much drink is OK. Remember, what happens in the mess stays in the mess and never comes back to haunt you on Monday morning!"

"Go on mate, marry her! You'll have a long, happy marriage, and of course she'll stay faithful while you're in the sandpit!"

"One for the road won't hurt... you've got another 15 minutes until the transport leaves..." Thanks for the walk, Emperor!

"That piece of Gucci kit will most certainly not make you look gay! Nor will it attract the attention of the RSM!"

"You will be on the beach 12 hours at most and back on the ship for tea and medals. Sleeping bag? Pah! You don't need one." 38 hours later I was still on the beach and still waiting. At least I had rations with me...

I'm sure the Emperor himself was working in the clothing store at Chilwell in 2003. He was the lying cnut who told me I would get my dessie combats in theatre.

"Just wear the feckers! Nobody will notice."

"There's bound to be a cashpoint/filling station in the next village." (There wasn't ... and there never is)

"Don't bother setting your alarm. Someone else is bound to get up before you." (They didn't)

"You had better pack an iron, nobody else will think of taking one. Take a kettle as well... go on." (Eight man room, eight men, eight kettles and eight irons!)

"It's only the north of Scotland, it's April and it won't be that cold." (Woke up to find ice on the tent, both inside and out, and the water for the tea had frozen, along with the milk!)

"Your name is not on the works ticket. If you just park the rover and hand in the keys they will never know it was you that bashed it while doing some personal off road training!"

Part 1

Signalman Peel (thinks): I'm sure I heard that when wiring these newfangled Wolf Land Rovers up to the radio batteries I must do it the opposite way round. No problem...

EM: Argh, what art thou doing?

Peel: Just wiring these batteries up – why?

EM: Verily, thou shalt blow thyself up if thou dost it that way.

Peel: No, no. I read it somewhere that...

EM: Dost thou doubt my word?

Peel: Of course not Your Mongesty, how could I?

(Cue fizzly pop and cloud of acrid smoke.)

Peel: Cnut!

Part 2 – In hospital

Peel: Fuck me I'm bored, hooked up to this heart monitor, due to my sudden electrical interface.

EM: Look what happens when you touch the electrode just so...

Peel: Why, it makes an extra beep on the heart monitor! How entertaining!

EM: Thou should do it some more, perhaps to the tune of "Match of ye Day".

Peel: I will, Your Mongesty!

(Signalman Peel proceeds to tap said electrode.)

Huge Klaxony thing: AWOOOOGA!

(Cue lots of running and shouting from the Cardiac Crash team. Peel sits shame-faced.)

Peel: Cnut!

Arms store, Ebrington Derry, 1985. It is 2359 hours and Corporal Palmer is bored shitless.

EM: On duty again Corporal Palmer?

Cpl Palmer: Yeah. Fucking extras again!

EM: So why not check that the lads have done their NSPs correctly by firing the action on this big rack of SLRs? The night will just fly past.

Cpl Palmer: Top idea, Exalted One! No wonder you run the universe with ideas like that.

Squeeze... no. Squeeze... no. Squeeze... click! Squeeze... no. Squeeze... no. Squeeze... BANG!

Palmer: Nooo!

EM: Mwahahahahahah!

EM: Look lad, she's gagging for it (tasty bit of totty at train station), go-on, give her all the patter, yes, I know the last train leaves in 20 minutes, but Troopy and the SSM aren't that bad, as long as you get back some time tomorrow you're not technically AWOL, just a little late...

Next day...

EM: Look lad, I know you didn't get laid (she must have been a lesbian) but look on the bright side – all your mates are off on a 10-mile 'welcome back from leave' run while you're relaxing in this very nice 8 x 4 foot cell. It's a shame that your depot cells were full, but I am sure these nice people with maroon berets will make you very welcome in their little guardroom for the next seven days. Relax! Have fun!

PUMA (Pilot Under Mong's Authority)

Fermanagh, Northern Ireland and a Geordie Colour Sergeant RGJ (who just happened to be a top Recce Platoon honcho who had previously navigated his entire Battle Group in BATUS, at night, hence knows how to read a map) is having a 'discussion' with the Crab pilot tasked with his team's insertion by Puma. Unfortunately for all, the Emperor Mong has tired of his usual squaddie targets, who in any case have developed a certain resistance since arriving in the Province, and has turned his attentions to the pilot.

Geordie: I think we're over the Border, like.

EM: (Speaking through the pilot) No, I don't think so.

Geordie: I think you'll fookin' find I'm right, like!

EM: Who's driving?

Geordie: Who's fookin' walkin' when we get oot, like?

EM: I know where I am!

Loady: Debus! We're here!

We duly debus amid huge clattering, etc, of large RAF thing. Silence on departure of said thing.

Geordie: We're on the wrong side of the border, like!

Boss: You're fucking joking!

Geordie: Am I fookin' laffin', like?

Eight of us look around and, yes, there is a white phone box with Telefon, etc... Rapid extraction commences.

Luckily it was but a kilometre and 0300 hours, but the large clattery crab thing had woken many. Op aborted.

Shoite to pay next day. Crab got RTU'd and how we laughed.

The Emperor Mong will ALWAYS prevail!

Wheelhouse Wallies

Emperor Mong has been serving afloat since Neanderthal man discovered he could sit on a floating log and paddle it with his hands. Mong has long since traded in his good conduct badges for a long service medal with many, many bars. Trafalgar, Jutland, the River Plate, Bluff Cove – Mong's No.1s hang heavy with campaign medals from all these places. Usually, he served with both sides at the same time.

As fans of films like *The Cruel Sea* will know, ships used to be controlled by an officer standing on the bridge and shouting orders into metal tubes. This wasn't some form of early, computer voice recognition. They were just metal tubes that ran through the ship and appeared somewhere that orders needed to be heard.

One of the tubes led to the 'wheelhouse' – an armoured, windowless compartment in the middle of the ship containing the ship's steering wheel, a gyro repeater to show the ship's course and absolutely nothing else. Except, that is, for a poor bastard with the worst job in the world: staring at the gyro repeater for hours on end and making small adjustments on the wheel to keep the repeater showing the ordered course. If you were unlucky, you'd get the middle watch – from midnight to 0400 hours – in the wheelhouse. If you were really unlucky your ship would be transiting the Pacific and the course wouldn't change for days at a time.

On one occasion, at about 0300 hours, the wheelhouse was occupied by the trusty coxswain, who handled the wheel with a masterly grip, and a cook of ill-repute who was at a loose end while the batch of tomorrow's bread he was baking was in the oven.

Despite having a combined IQ that was lower than some of the marine invertebrates fouling the ship's hull, this pair were easily bored. As they say, the Emperor makes work for idle hands and they soon discovered that the bolt securing the ship's wheel was loose. Not only could the bolt be unscrewed, but the entire wheel could be removed – thus leaving a 2,500 ton warship doing up to 20 knots and containing 300+ mainly sleeping matelots totally out of control.

A new form of entertainment was born (no ipods, playstations or DVDs in those days). The pair of loons took turns unbolting the wheel and then bolting it back on again. The 'winner' of the game was the one who needed to apply the smallest course correction after reattaching the wheel.

Like all games, this one soon became boring, so to spice things up a bit they decided that they would run round the wheelhouse, carrying the wheel, before reattaching it.

In time, this too became boring. To cut a long story a bit shorter, they ended up unbolting the wheel and running round the entire upper deck (that's the main, outside 'floor' of the ship that has the big guns, superstructure and helicopters parked on it) while carrying the wheel, before returning to the wheelhouse and reattaching it.

As I said, they were not burdened by the ravages of intelligence. It didn't occur to either of them that, at all times when the ship was at sea, the bridge was occupied by an Officer of the Watch (OOW) who was selected for having near perfect eyesight and whose powers of observation were honed by years of training. Naturally, the OOW this particular night was somewhat perturbed to see some foul creature scurrying across the fo'csle (the pointy bit at the front) in the small hours of the morning carrying a large object of indeterminate origin.

Three swift steps and the OOW was on the bridge wing (an open 'balcony' at each side of the bridge). With the flick of a switch he activated the searchlight and illuminated the miscreant, who froze like the protagonist in a comedy jailbreak.

The shouted conversation went like this:

OOW: Who the fuck is that on the fo'csle?

Cox'n: Nobody sir.

OOW: Is that you coxswain? Jesus Christ! Who's steering the ship?

Cox'n: Err...

OOW: What's that you're carrying?

Cox'n: Nothing sir.

OOW: It looks like ... JESUS FUCKING CHRIST – IT'S THE SHIP'S WHEEL!

The ship's company were promptly roused to their emergency stations (the bits of the ship where they go in an emergency such as a fire, a hull breach or a mad bastard nicking the main steering gear).

The Captain, on hearing the pipe for emergency stations, promptly ran up the bridge ladder in his pyjamas, fearing that his ship had been torpedoed by a rogue Nazi submarine that didn't know WW2 had ended or a rogue commie submarine that didn't know WW3 had yet to begin.

The ship's wheel was reattached, the off-duty crew returned to their bunks and calm returned to all parts of the ship. Except, that is, to the part occupied by the Captain, who was crazed by a furious rage.

At that time, the Naval Discipline Act still allowed the death penalty in some circumstances. The regulators (naval military police) were kept up all night investigating whether this was one of those circumstances and whether the Captain could, through some obscure legal loophole, award a death sentence at the end of a summary trial (where the Captain is the judge and jury and usually hands out a fine).

Not wanting to damage the ship's new fangled radar and sensitive antennae, the Captain quickly ruled out hanging and made enquiries among the Royal Marines about the possibility of a firing squad on the quarterdeck (the flat bit at the back of the ship – usually occupied by a knackered, 25-year-old helicopter on modern RN ships).

Sadly, the Captain's hopes of conducting the first summary execution aboard ship since Private John Dalinger RM met his maker in 1860 were to be dashed. He had to make do with Courts Martial, discharge and hefty jail sentences for the hapless coxswain and hopeless cook (whose bread ignited during the aftermath of the incident and brought the crew, once more, to emergency stations).

So remember, when Mong speaks to you, think of the consequences. Being reamed by the Captain is far, far less of an ordeal than being reamed by your cell mate when Emperor Mong lands you in Wormwood Scrubs for two years.

A Squaddie Unmasked

Bravely and without thought for safety, the shiny truck was driven from Antrim to Belfast to deliver unto the construction team much needed supplies of steel mesh and girders. Armed only with a 9mm pistol, two Yorkie bars and a copy of the previous day's *Sun*, the driver and his companion had steered the vehicle through bad places, pretending to be civilians. As the finely disguised lorry was being disgorged of its load, the fearless pair retired to the canteen to partake of more fat- drenched trukkie treats.

In the canteen, L/Cpl Barnes was himself taking a well-earned tea break to quench his parched throat after many hours of electrically welding girders in shock-inducing torrential rain. Pleasantries and verbal insults were exchanged before Barnes was offered the tatty and much-pawed copy of the army's favourite rag to peruse. Deep in concentration somewhere between pages 2 and 4, he failed to notice that, in retaliation for a previous jape, the civilianised driver was very carefully writing in chalk the word 'knobber' on the rear of his flak-collecting jacket.

As Barnes dragged himself back out to the rain-drenched construction site that had previously been a tidy-looking RUC station, at which point there was much tittering and noises of merriment from his rear. Kindly, and after only two hours or so, a fellow welder pointed out the graffiti added to the bullet-stopping attire. Very grumpily, the insulting slogan was scrubbed from the jacket. But how to recover from this insult and achieve revenge? How to regain honour and cause the insolent truckkie to be equally slighted?

Cue arrival on site of his mighty eminence, King of the Worthless and Emperor of all that is Mongness.

EM: Oh foolish child with one stripe of rank; how ridiculous the steerer of large vehicles has made you appear! And he with no stripe or privilege! You must return the jape, and quickly, or there will be months of 'knobber' name-calling from all those who munch upon Yorkies and eat pies.

L/Cpl Barnes : But how will I strike quickly oh great Lord?

EM: Fool! Here, take this chalk and writeth in large letters the word 'SQUADDIE' upon the driver's door of the great truck ... and a little arrow pointing up to the window.

Barnes: But, Lord of the Worthless, Protector of the Great Extra Duties Jape, the truck is mightily civilianised, it is new and shiny and they have a perilous journey to complete in the land of the rock thrower.

EM: You truly are a 'knobber' and undeserving of my time. The one who aims the truck, the failer of all Battle Fitness Tests, the tormentor of Godly welders of higher rank and esteem, will notice the chalk marked insult and will be forced to clean it off in front of the assembled and mocking field mice.

Barnes: But mighty one, the chalk that you offer is road chalk, which is hard to remove and will be sharp against the pristine paintwork of the mighty lorry.

EM: Get on with it you metal-joining toad! Before they return from their pie-eating feast.

And so the jape was done. Large letters forming the word 'SQUADDIE' were inscribed on the driver's door of the new truck along with a little arrow pointing up to the window, after which L/Cpl Barnes was sent to the other side of the site to weld.

In the terrible rain, neither the driver nor his companion noticed the new slogan added to the vehicle and nobody else sought to tell them as they left the sanctuary of the police station. Within two minutes of departing, they stopped at traffic lights which glowed red, near a school in a fiercely Republican area at the exact time that the fierce children were swarming from the gates to return home after a fierce day's tuition.

They *did* see the words and many large lumps of masonry and other brickwork and debris and bottles containing paint were projected onto the vehicle, causing its shiny livery to change and large dents to appear, thus forcing the truck to flee from the scene, speeding through the still-red lights and clipping a car.

They arrived back in Antrim, fearful and much-panicked due to the unknown cause of the compromise ... and then the words upon the door were discovered. The MT Sergeant and the Sergeant Major entered into great discussions with the OC and L/Cpl Barnes was summoned back to Antrim to face the wrath of wiser men with more than one stripe of rank and much cash was later removed from his wages.

Not satisfied with this victory, the Emperor was to visit L/Cpl Barnes again, and again, and again, no matter what stripes of rank he wore!

April Fool Fiasco

As the Regiment deployed on the Divisional exercise, the newly-promoted Corporal Barnes sat back at the desk in the guard-room, knowing that he was in Easy Strasse for the next two weeks. Easy, but boring strasse! Not a lot to do, no prisoner to beast and no need for the daily, mindless, wander around camp with the RSM looking for offensive long grass, unpainted concrete and recently discarded fag butts. What to do to amuse himself then?

A flash of inspiration as the mighty Conscienceless One enters the guardroom:

EM: Oh minute testicular fool, I see you are now of two stripes? You are progressing well, small brain.

CPL Barnes: Your Un-nicely Meanness, short time no see! Yes, I am now of two stripes of greatness but not doing as well as you point out: one stripe for 7 years after the unfeasibly crap CR following the great 'Covert Truck Jape' you talked me into. Are you here to further hamper my career?

EM: Not at all, dear naivety. I am here merely to enhance your duty. In short, to bring light and fun into your miserable existence. With a jape! A jape that will have all rolling with laughter at your simple brilliance.

Barnes: So what do you plan, your Royal Lunacy?

EM: Is tomorrow not the day of great jape? The very first of April, when humour can be had at the expense of a fool? And is not the Adjutant in charge of things until he of greater rank returns from the field? And is the Adjutant, in your opinion, of great education yet small mind?

Barnes: Well, I may have thought that in the past. But, your serene Career-Endingness, is not the Adjutant already opposed to me? Has he not already mentioned that he has my 'card marked' when, as the Int NCO, I changed all the codes to the safes so he couldn't get in during the security inspection? You remember, just before I went on leave?

EM: Bah, he loved that jape really! He didn't charge you did he? Just a few extra duties was all! Well worth the recognition as the Regimental Japester.

Barnes: But what about when my troop commander was dog sitting the Adjutants' black Labrador for the weekend? I'm convinced he knows it was me who kidnapped it and painted it with gloss paint to resemble a Dalmatian!

EM: Dim-witted dunderhead! Did he not give the extras to troopy?

Barnes: OK, you're right. What is the jape this time mighty Trickster and taker of career stripes?

EM: Well, you know how as Int NCO you had the two Soviet uniforms made? And you know how the CO's car, an Opal Senator, very much resembles a SOXMIS car? This very evening employ your friend, the Regimental Draughtsman, to make fake SOXMIS number plates to fit on the CO's car. On the morrow dress two men as Soviet Soldiers and get them to park the car outside RHQ, dismount and take photographs. Perfect for 1st April and perfect for the Emperor Mong's Day.

And so, the jape was done. Early on the morrow, as NAAFI break approached, there was an appearance of a SOXMIS car outside RHQ and two fake Soviets did dismount and freely take photographs for 15 minutes, whereupon the Adjutant appeared and called for his gun-wielding guard, just as the fake Soviets leapt into the car to escape, whereafter the Light Wheeled Tractor driver did try (unsuccessfully) to ram the SOXMIS car with forks raised high and the civilian coach driver did swerve his 40-seater to (successfully) ram the SOXMIS car, whereupon Corporal Barnes did have to leap bodily in front of a young Sapper as he raised his cocked SLR to kill the invading Soviet child-killers.

The Adjutant was unforgiving when he realised that it was a jape and spake unto Corporal Barnes that many wise men of much higher esteem than one with two stripes would request his presence in two weeks and that, once again, money would be extracted from his wages and another crap CR would follow.

Nevertheless, the Emperor Mong would appear again to the fool who wished to progress in greatness of stripes!

16. Mick, Mac, Paddy, Wack – Give The Lad A Name

Here we include a collection of the finest nicknames that serving and former members of the Armed Forces have been proud to answer to, plus some coined by their mates that they may prefer to forget! Nowhere near an exhaustive list, there are many more in use, but dozens are invented each week as the Emperor Mong applies his mischief or Ball & Chain antics are acted out.

50 Hertz Hodge

This bloke must be out now but was an apprentice in Harrogate in 1980... It came about during a big exercise; you know the type, all comms and combat. Go out and let the DS mess you around for 3 or 4 days. Many will be familiar with the pattern: move into a location, get the comms in, wagons cammed up, bashers erected. Start settling in to be told it is shite and get ordered to de-cam and move on to a new location 20 feet away. 'Stand To' as it gets dark, then a bit later the enemy attack. Defend with SLRs and blanks. DS come, decide it's crap again so move another 20 feet! This goes on for two days or so. Also have DS inspections every morning for clean weapons, mess tins, etc.

The hero of the tale knew all about the exercise plan and decided to do something about it with a plan of his own.

1. No need to clean the gat if it's never fired. As all the attacks are at night the DS won't see anything. Pop down to Woolworths buy the biggest, loudest cap-firing pistol available. DS will hear bang, see flash and all Ok. Shiny, clean gat on inspection.

2. Mess tins had to be clean inside and out, not easy after cooking on hexy. Easy. Pop down to the co-op and buy six Pot Noodles. All you need is hot water. After eating, bin the empty plastic pots. Shiny mess tins for the inspection.

3. Hot water? No problem; the wagons have 240v AC. Just need a heating device. Back down to Woolworths and buy a single-cup heating element. While there, also buy a small reading lamp and plug and socket to make up a power lead for the basher (all forbidden, of course).

On the night of the exercise, deploy, set up, bugger about, move, set up, Stand To ... all going to plan. Move twice more. Gets dark.

Time to make the power lead. No flat twin available. No problem; use D10. Unspool some from the wagon. But it's all in short lengths. The basher is 15m away. Our hero has a 7m and an 8m length. No crimping tool though. No worries. Remembering his Basic Signalling skills he recalls that you can join D10 with a knot. Shit, no harry maskers! No problem; just offset the knots by 2cm so they wont short out. Plug in, lay line to basher. Jump into maggot and have a brew. Hide under maggot with lamp waiting for the next Stand To with cap gun in one hand whilst studying Miss April 1982 with the other.

Stand To, bells and whistles. Our hero jumps up. Can't see a bloody thing as it's pitch black outside and he's lost all his night vision. No worries – he uses the D10 as a guideline. What he doesn't know is that the DS are in the back of his wagon. He stumbles along for 6.95m then his clammy wet 5cm hand crosses the 240v AC join in the cable. He gets the first belt of 240v, starts screaming, thrashing around on the floor and firing his cap gun. Inside the wagon the lights flicker and dim and then the ELCB trips.

The DS hear all the noise but now just a low moaning can be heard. But the DS don't like being in the dark do they! They reset the ELCB – power back on. Outside hero boy is still clutching the D10 in one hand and his cap gun in the other. Second belt of 240v and the screams and rapid firing start again. DS get out of wagon to see AT Hodge writhing on the ground firing has cap gun as his muscles spasm.

DS collapse in a heap laughing as ELCB trips again. Hodge is taken to Ripon casualty and for him the exercise is over.

From then on the story of "50 Hertz Hodge" is used as a warning to all ATs not to be a smart-arse whilst on exercise.

Jones 125

As 2IC Guard for a Welsh regiment I was sorting out the stags, and half the Guard were called Jones, one of whom I knew was 'Jones 125', so I stuck his name and 'last three' down, but he piped up that 125 was not his last three.

He explained that he had been on an Inter City 125 train that did not stop at the station he wanted to get off at, so out went his kitbag and he followed! Luckily, he only broke half the bones in his body and the head injury missed his brain by 5'9". Hence the new last 3 and the nickname – Jones 125!

Eddie

We had a lad in our Unit who we called 'Eddie'. His name was Kennedy and one morning, whilst on parade, the SSM had called out to him "Kennedy, what's your last three?"

"E.D.Y." came the reply!

Plug

An Int Corps bloke posted into 3 Div in the early 80s found that he needed a different type of plug on his electric razor, so he popped down the Gadaffi and bought a 2-pin. He then proceeded to chop the old plug off and wire the new one on. Five minutes later he was left with an electric razor that still didn't work and a piece of wire with a 2-pin plug on one end and a 3-pin plug on the other. 'Plug' was born!

Mop & Bucket

Two local lasses from the choice drinking establishments of Munster were known as "Mop & Bucket" cos they'd been up &

down every corridor in every accommodation block in Loddenhiede...

Turbo

'Turbo' was an affectionate name given to an AGC TA clerk in Kosovo in 2002. Case study:

1. After twenty minutes of cursing at photocopier, frantically pressing start and nothing happening, a new Sapper walks past and flicks the power switch at the wall.
2. Ran out of paper for photocopier and asked me where she could get some more. I told her to "Ring RHQ up at main and get them to fax you some through." She did!

Dipstick

OK, he was straight out the factory at the time, but we were waiting to deploy on exercise and Geordie had taken three quarters of an hour ago to top up the oil on the OC TP Rover. Sent to find him, I discovered him down at MT with a polystyrene cup with a hole in the bottom, filled with oil, which he is watching dribble down the dipstick hole!

"WTF are you doing Geordie? The OC is waiting!"

"Not ma fecking fault," Geordie replies. "The oil won't go doon any faster and I couldnae find anything wi a small enough spout to fill it wi'out spilling oil all over the place!

Chock

In Catterick we had a driver who once had a problem driving a JCB up the hill from camp centre in the Richmond direction. The thing just clapped out before it got to the top of the hill so he jumped out to see what the problem was. Due to faulty brakes, or whatever, the JCB began to roll backwards down the hill. As it started to move, the driver tried to jump in to stop it, but slipped on the steps and was pinned by one of the front wheels. He wasn't too badly hurt, and he did stop the JCB from

destroying Lloyds Bank or the barbers at the bottom of the hill...
From then on he was known as 'Chock'.

Others – Short and Sharp

PONTI: Person of No Tactical Importance. Invented and used by front-line troops during Gulf War 1 when everyone was ordered not to use **REMF** (Rear Echelon Mother Fucker) for those way behind the front lines, as it was lowering morale!

Pen Knife: A useless tool that everyone carries.

Vic: Gets up everyone's nose.

Thrush: An irritating little cnut.

Gerber: A Complete Tool.

Tracer: On a BFT he used to burn out after 1100m.

Exocet: You can see him coming but there's fuck all you can do about it and he's sure to ruin your week.

FUMIN: Fucking Ugliest Man in NATO.

Hesco Bastion: Full of crap and difficult to get rid of.

Biscuit: Crumbles under pressure.

Kipper: Two-faced and spineless.

Baggage: Always being carried.

Ug: Surname 'Lee'.

Turtles: Surname 'Head'.

CS: A fast acting irritant.

Whiskers: Breath smelt of cat food.

Camnet: Useless in camp and annoying on exercise.

Squid: He was spineless!

Harry: Surname 'Black'.

ZULU: An hour behind everyone else.

NoSmo: Surname 'King'.

Santa: Only did one day's work a year.

Drill Bit: A boring tool.

Brains: Anyone with spectacles (after *Thunderbirds* puppet).

Coolant: Had an IQ of minus 37.

Sizzler: When he spoke, he spat like a pan of bacon.

nimdA: His admin was backwards.

17. Talking Out of Your ARRSE

The aim of ARRSE (Army RumouR ServicE) – in so far that it has one – was to provide a useful, informative and amusing site for people with an interest in the British Army. Contrary to duty rumour, they are not promoting the overthrow of Her Majesty's Government, nor do they exist to toe the Party Line. Users can expect to find both reasoned argument and complete ARRSE within their pages. The site exists for all. With the very kind permission of Good & Bad COs (the ARRSE owners) we have been able to put this chapter together. Thanks to them both & to the ARRSE members who penned the following classics. (from Arrsepedia)

ARRSE Daffynitions

Officers

Theory: Acting as both leaders and managers, officers are the people responsible for the welfare of soldiers in the British Army. It's down to officers to make the most of their team's unique talents, bring out the best in them in any situation and hold them together when the pressure's on – even in a war setting.

Reality: Officers just ponce about a lot, shout "Hurrah", wear trousers with offensively loud colours and get naked a lot in the Officers Mess bar. Sooner or later they get promoted to such ridiculous levels of responsibility that the better ones just leave everything alone so the NCOs can run things smoothly while others insist on playing with their train-sets and buggering everything up for generations to come.

Young Officers often behave as if still at university, frittering away their salaries on SOUPs (Single Officers' Useless Purchases) until they meet a bird they've shagged often enough to want to settle down and get married. Eventually they marry a horsey-type called Fenella who has a thing for Hermes scarves and tweed. Accompanied by 2.4 kids, a Labrador and a battered Volvo they often owe over half their salary to the bank and have dreams of retiring to a sheep farm in Wales where their memoirs can be written.

Sergeants

First level of SNCO, can be found at Platoon and Squadron level tidying up after the Subalterns' accidents. That nice NCO who always thinks of great new ways to get you running. The rank after Corporal and before Staff Sergeant in the British and US Armies. Often mistakenly abbreviated to *Sarge* instead of *Sar'nt*. This is normally a mistake new Officer Cadets and Privates make ... once!

Corporals

Often abbreviated to Cpl. A 'Full Screw' normally commands a section. He or she is usually found on exercise being shouted at by a subaltern who has no idea why the shouting occurs. A Section Commander:
- Will receive orders at the Platoon Commander's O Group.
- Will prepare and deliver said orders to his section, who will have no idea what he is on about.
- Will generally resort to simple commands e.g. 'follow me!'

Generally regarded as being the best rank to be – high enough to have authority and delegate the bone jobs, but low enough to still be at the coalface, having all the fun before you become an adult! The Section Commander (a.k.a. Sexual Banana) is in general a nasty hard-arsed Corporal that commands the Section.

In the infantry, the role of the section is to deliver the Section Commander onto the enemy so that he can get amongst them and cause havoc and kill, "Like what they pay you for." (C Sgt Bourne in *Zulu*). Section Commanders should be kept in locked boxes marked "to be used only in time of war" but sadly they aren't.

Privates

Private is the lowest rank in the British Army and the most important one. They have the potential to be enriched and developed into fighting men and women. They are the stem cells (or possibly, more accurately, bacteria) of the British Army.

The Squaddie

The word is often used as a term of abuse by civilians and members of the RAF, who frankly don't know their Dr Johnson: "Every man thinks meanly of himself for not having been a soldier, or not having been at sea." This famous 18th century wit and man of letters clearly knew his British Armed Forces (and you'll notice he has nothing good to say about the RAF!).

When a civilian joins the Army, he or she becomes a 'squaddie'. After their service is terminated they seldom return to Civvy Street in their former guise and are transformed into 'ex-squaddies' rather than civilians, although this rather depends on their individual service experience. Those with positive experiences show pride in the term, whereas those with an axe to grind or something to hide might choose not to be associated with the Army and thus not refer to themselves as an 'ex-squaddie'.

A squaddie is not a role or position as such; it's a state of mind. There are two basic people types: Squaddies and non-Squaddies (civvies). Many civvies show signs of squaddiedom (such as drinking to excess, masturbating regularly and telling sick jokes) but unless you serve you can never truly be referred as a squaddie.

Please note that the title squaddie is not given on learning the Basics or on Passing Out, but after a period of *bezzing* and *skiffing* within the Regiment.

A Squaddie can best be summed up by the infamous quote by Sir Arthur Wellesley, Duke of Wellington, who said of them:

"I don't know what effect these men will have upon the enemy, but, by God, they frighten me!"

The Sleeping Bag (aka Green Maggot)

Worthy of mention as the soldier spends as much 'down' time as possible in one. Once a soldier is in one of these, it can be hard to extract him. After a year or two, the average army sleeping bag contains enough of a soldier's DNA to construct an exact 1/6th scale replica. Often can be found to contain a well-used wank sock!

Survive to Fight

One of the finest works of literary fantasy the world has ever witnessed is *Survive to Fight* – the booklet issued to all soldiers detailing what to do in case of nuclear, biological or chemical attack. The cover featured a NBC suited & booted soldier – complete with S6 and SLR – charging, bayonet fixed, towards his inevitable demise at the hands of the 3rd Shock Army.

Frankly if they had just written, *'YOU'RE ALL GOING TO DIE'* on the front it would have saved both time and money.

The contents were:

Immediate Action Drill – Nuclear

Sadly, the correct drill for actions when a Nuke gets dropped was omitted – so here it is:
1. Lie down somewhere comfortable.
2. Tuck your head firmly between your legs.
3. Kiss your arse goodbye.
4. Die.

Immediate Action Drill – Biological

The 'biological' aspect has never been adequately explained, as there's nothing really instantaneous about being eaten inside out by the Ebola virus, so its tactical use is negligible. However:
1. Carry on as normal.

2. Collapse six weeks later.
3. Die.

Immediate Action Drill – Chemical

The 'chemical' bit is more likely, very nasty and more frightening than the 'bucket of sunshine' option. Not to worry, *Survive to Fight* covers every aspect of what to do upon hearing GAS! GAS! GAS! or your NAIAD chirruping merrily, including how to operate and live in a poisoned environment – right down to the infamous 'Task 17'.

1. Shit yourself – paying no attention to the procedure laid out in Task 17.
2. Mask in 9 (seconds) and realise some cnut has nicked your filter. See above.
3. Wonder why everything is becoming blurred.
4. Cough.
5. Splutter.
6. Fall over.
7. Have an eppy.
8. And... you've guessed it. Die. (Is there a pattern emerging here?)

Task 17

Task 17[12] is legendary. I suppose this specific drill can also be used for knocking one out under NBC Black; not that I have tried it – or know of anyone else who has been insane or desperate enough to attempt it!

---

[12] Task 17: Defecation drills. Other drills seem logical enough, and are well practised but, considering the risks, we feel this one really is a load of shite. Bring on the compo and constipation! Possible alternative uses, as it has potential to be used for any activity requiring access to the genitalia.

50 Little-Known Facts about the SAS

1. All UK pubs are required by law to have one alcoholic regular who used to be a member of the SAS and was 2nd Man on the Balcony at the Iranian Embassy Siege.

2. During selection, potential SAS recruits are required to bite the head off a live ferret – except in *Dog Soldiers,* where they have to shoot a live dog!

3. All SAS men must now sign a contract agreeing never to disclose anything about their service, never to call any officer 'Sir' and never to trim their moustaches.

4. The wine served in both messes at Stirling Lines (complete with winged dagger SAS motif wine label) is, in fact, cheap German wine purchased from the local Netto.

5. Inside the Sergeants Mess, in a glass case, is a dressed-up mannequin in genuine Iranian Embassy garb! Only it's not a mannequin. It is, in fact, none other than Lofty Wiseman, who is paid to stand in the glass case completely still from 12.30pm until the bar closes around midnight. He is entitled to free food and refreshments in the bar too.

6. They are vulnerable to kryptonite, but only during a full moon.

7. Since *Dog Soldiers* came out, all SAS weapons are loaded with silver bullets in case they meet real werewolves.

8. David Stirling, the SAS founder, had a pet hamster called Bismark.

9. Someone called Andy McNab now runs an Anne Summers franchise in Brighton.

10. Trooper Jimbo 'The Hatchet' Johnson's autobiography *On The Piss In Hereford* has been turned down by 37 publishers.

11. My Dad was in the SAS.

12. During the Malayan Emergency the SAS were known by the Communist guerrillas as 'The Moustaches from Hell'.

13. The Sultan of Oman owes the SAS a few beers – probably a brewery – and an ale named after them too. "A pint of Special Ale Service please barman" sounds good to me anyway.

14. The SAS spelt backwards is SAS.

15. The real Iranian Embassy siege only lasted two minutes. The TV footage was a dramatised re-enactment for the cameras.

16. During the Falklands conflict the SAS pioneered the use of specially-trained exploding penguins.

17. In the first Gulf War the SAS pioneered the use of laser-guided specially-trained exploding 'smart' camels.

18. The SAS are wanted for questioning by the World Wildlife Fund, the RSPCA and David Attenborough.

19. 'A Fresher Sod' is an anagram of SAS Hereford.

20. SAS is an anagram of ASS.

21. The SAS drink Scrumpy. Lots of it.

22. The SAS drink anything. Lots of it.

23. The Australian SAS have a mounted Kangaroo Squadron.

24. The Iranian SAS don't exist.

25. More soldiers have been RTU'd from Hereford than have actually served in the army since 1624.

26. Colour blindness is reason for RTU, as not correctly quoting the colour of the Boathouse is a security breach.

27. SAS soldiers carry a tampon with them in their first aid pack. It has many uses.

28. SAS soldiers also carry condoms for water collection in an emergency. Allegedly.

29. The SAS selection process includes escaping in a Mondeo through a chemical plant full of obstacles. Hardly fair for those who have no driving licence.

30. The SAS are famous for the 'double-tap'. This is where they tap you on the shoulder not once, but twice to gain your attention.

31. The Polish SAS are also famous for 'double-taps'. They are all cross-trained as plumbers.

32. It is claimed that the SAS are so well-trained in covert operations, that a single soldier can steal a 24 pack of Wifebeater from Netto, drink it, and put the empty box back before anyone notices it's gone.

33. Instead of 'biscuits brown' SAS members receive two packets of Iced Gems in their specially-made ration packs.

34. Amongst their most famous ex-members is The Leprechaun of Death.

35. The SAS have an OP watching Gray's Lane, Ashtead. It's still there in case the NIMBYs get snotty again.

36. SAS men are trained to eat Ferrero Rocher at Ambassadors' receptions without attracting attention.

37. The SAS and their sister organisation the SBS are blamed for the Army-wide shortage of 'Black Nasty', the tape they use to cover their eyes when photographers are around.

38. The tabloid rumours about the SAS almost catching Bin Laden in the Tora Boras are actually all true. Afterwards, the President personally phoned the SAS squad in the mountains and told them to wait for the US Marines. The SAS decided to go into the caves and challenge Bin Laden and his Al Qaeda cronies to a game of cribbage. Luckily, Colour Sergeant Mabelle Farthington, the first 65 year-old woman allowed to join the elite unit, had just competed in a tournament at the Credenhill Village Hall where she was

announced cribbage champion of Herefordshire County. Safe to say, Mabelle was up for the challenge and Bin Laden suffered a devastating defeat. Unfortunately, Bin Laden escaped unnoticed while Mabelle shuffled cards for the next round. He has not been seen since, but – some believe he died from humiliation shortly after the ordeal.

39. The highest rate of service divorce is attributed to the SAS, with spouses often blaming the training. Several wives said, "Our sex life is rubbish. He is trained to get in and out without anyone noticing, including me!"

40. A certain number of ex-SAS men meet once a year to discuss book deals and creative writing styles. Head of the Long Page Literary Group (LPLG) was unable to attend the last meeting as he had severe pen flash: a type of burn from writing so much, so quickly.

41. During *Desert Storm*, one sergeant who led an ill-fated patrol was once heard to say, "The pen is mightier than the M16 203".

42. The SAS is so hard that *Ultimate Force* DVDs can double as ballistic plates ... no, seriously!

43. SAS selection is not the British Army's hardest course to pass. The catering course is. To date no-one has passed.

44. The lads NEVER discuss operations in pubs and clubs around the city of Hereford. I have never heard them do so and would not know what to listen out for either.

45. Teams of four, eight and sometimes twelve guys do not go on the piss and pose around, making it obvious just who they are.

46. They do not try to out psyche anybody foolish enough to stare at them and they never ever wear discrete but oh so obvious military hardware that just cannot be obtained anywhere else except from the QM's stores up at the base!

All this is strictly tongue in cheek by the way. Love ya really guys. It's just that most of us – after military service – just faded into the background and got on with the rest of our lives!

47. Contrary to popular belief, SQMS in 'Them' do not issue long droopy moustaches along with MP5s – this has to be 'grown'. But the moustache will only grow once the trooper has evaded capture for three months or longer.

48. All ex 'Them' do not drive round their local village in '90 landies' sliding round corners into parking slots then diving from their vehicles into a perfect forward roll, just to post a letter to their mums.

49. Contrary to popular belief, 'They' do stag like everyone else. 'They' can sometimes be seen wandering aimlessly (in slow motion) around the perimeter fence in groups of four or six – in full black rig – with shotguns over their shoulders. Sometimes encountered on the pan for no apparent reason, complete with background music.

50. There are at least five undercover SAS operatives signing on at any UK Job Centre, each using a different well known SAS alias. At least two of them will confess to being 'second man on the balcony' on any job application form.

*Reproduced by kind permission of **ARRSE** – the Online Home of the British Soldier & former Soldier – **www.arrse.co.uk***

18. You Know You're a Squaddie When...

Having worked dutifully through the preceding chapters, some serving or former soldiers may be in doubt about their 'squaddiness'. Some out-and-out civilians may have difficulty in relating to the tales, or in understanding the squaddie mentality. For the former, we offer this chapter of diagnostic tools. To the latter, commiserations; you are missing out on one of life's motherlodes of humour. We can offer encouragement to keep trying, but no advice on the path to enlightenment.

You know you're a Squaddie / have been Defence institutionalised or are/were a Soldier when...

- You use target indication to point out hot chicks.

- You use the term 'chicks'.

- You insist on dancing like a dick, whilst your civvy mates insist on trying to dance 'properly'.

- Your civvy mates don't understand any of the terminology you use such as 'no dramas', 'squared away', 'take a knee' etc.

- You can't help saying 'Roger', 'Say again' and other snappy bits of VP.

- You use acronyms thinking your civvy mates will understand what you are talking about.

- You don't have any civvy mates.

- You cringe, and mutter under your breath 'haircut', when you see men with long hair.

- You walk at a ridiculous pace and are physically incapable of walking at the shopping pace of your girlfriend.

- You refer to personal organisation as 'admin'.

- Your girlfriend is stored in your mobile phone address book as 'Zero Alpha'.

- You use patrol hand signals in a night club if people can't hear you.

- You always use the 24-hour clock.

- Nothing soldiers do shocks you any more.

- You can't watch war movies without giving a running commentary.

- People in prison have more contact with women than you do.

- Whenever you spell something out you use the phonetic alphabet.

- You don't trust your mum/wife/girlfriend/any woman to iron your kit because deep down you think that your ironing is better.

- You point using your whole hand in a karate chop motion.

- You find that the conversation somehow always comes back round to you, because you're more interesting than most topics of conversation.

- You think not shaving is a treat.

- You get really irritated when people you don't know call you 'mate'.

- You can read a junk mail catalogue from cover to cover and refer to everything that is useful as 'a Gucci bit of kit'.

- You refer to smoke as 'a double-edged sword'.

- You spend hours wondering where in civvie street you can get an equal disposable income and at least 6 weeks holiday a year, by completing an inversely proportionally tiny amount of tangible work.

- Your blood boils when you see civvies wearing DPM.

- Going out on Thursday 'international army night out' wherever it may be, or whichever course one is on, involves forming the ring-of-steel, talking about yourselves and the army and aggressively staring at girls, who if they don't immediately come over are obviously lesbians.

- Should any man dare break this ritual, and despite talking to the prettiest of girls – as we would like to do, if it weren't for the fact we tend to chew our own tongues and dribble – he is clearly gay!

- You come out in a cold sweat if you find yourself still working after lunch on a Friday...

- You have to stop work at 10am for NAAFI break or else you might not make it to lunch...

- At least half of your DVD collection is war movies...

- Even though your disposable income is twice that of a civvy you still manage to spend it all, every month, with nothing to show for it, about a week after you've told all your soldier colleagues that you 'can't believe how much money they waste on the urine'.

- You feel guilty about wearing jeans in front of senior officers in the mess.

- The sight of rolling countryside makes you scan for 'enemy in depth'.

- You think that eating every meal for a week with the same spoon that you licked clean and kept in the pocket of the same shirt you've worn all week is perfectly normal.

- All of your food has to be prepared by a chef because you're incapable of cooking anything that can't either be boiled in a bag or eaten cold.

- You lie when people ask you what you do for a living.

- When leaving your phone number on a voice message you can't just give it once, it has to be repeated.

- When surveying open ground (when not looking for enemy in depth) you think 'good tank country'. If a forestry block 'I could get a platoon in here'.

- You survey open ground.

- When you are pointing out some natural feature you begin with 'Reference bushy topped tree', etc, etc.

- Your girlfriend has started saying 'admin' and gave you the 'chop' when telling you to put the bin out.

- When meeting mates in a pub you always turn up 5 minutes early and are secretly angry that nobody else has. Worse still, if it's a venue you haven't been to before, you turn up 15 minutes early to put in a CTR, in order that you are definitely there 5 minutes early.

- You subconsciously red-pen everything you read.

- On a Friday at 12.15 your troop/platoon Sgt/Ssgt tells you that you are on exercise on Sunday afternoon for the next 3 weeks.

- You turn up for work and find out you are now on the squadron basketball team and you have an inter-squadron competition in 30 minutes even though you're 5ft tall and have never played basketball in your life. Or you turn up for PT thinking it's sport and it turns out to be a PFT, BFT, APFT or whatever they are calling it this week

- You hear yourself say 'right guys take a quick five minute break'. What the hell is a long five minute break? Five minutes is five minutes!

- Every time you see a Yorkie bar you feel cold and wet.

- Your Other Half tells you she has arranged a special treat for you – a three-course meal with all the trimmings at Brown's Restaurant – and you tell her thanks, but you would much rather stay at home and have a banquet of 3 egg banjos, babies' heads (tinned individual steak and kidney puddings) and a yellow handbag of Herforder Pils Beer

- You feel uneasy about walking on grass

- You always say 'Fancy a brew?' rather than a cuppa, coffee or Tea, etc

- A Map of Africa doesn't mean a Geographical layout of one of the main Continents, but actually something very damp and a lot closer to home

- You have still got an SSVC direct debit coming out of your account for £16 after ten years of paying for a TV & Video which you no longer have

- You wear a t-shirt and jeans to a nightclub and every time wonder why they won't let you in

- You use the term 'minutes, few' to describe how long you'll be

- Someone calls you and you reply with SEND

- When the worst phrase in the world is... – Wake Up You're on stag!

- You wake up the next morning and not know which country you're even in!

- You walk 'in-step' with your mates without realizing it

- All your going out shirts have razor creases in the arms cause it's the only way you know how to iron a shirt!

- After you have left and while working on contract in foreign climes – you still do all your own ironing 'cos the 'chogie' down the road can't iron like you, even though it only costs a pittance for him to do your entire locker-full.

- Getting out of a vehicle you catch yourself doing 5s and then 20s.

- You like to sit in the bar with your back against the wall, so you can scope out all the exits – you've made your extraction plan before you've sat down.

- You give an impromptu lesson on how to search a car to the security guard at the local hotel…

- You point out all the mistakes in a war movie… 'that would never happen because'…

- You think it weird when family members and civvy friends ask you to pass the knife, fork & spoon when all you can see is a set of diggers!

- You can spot every Squaddie in each bar and club and your civvy mates have no idea how you can do this

- Waking up next to the fattest female in town after a night on the lash makes you a legend among your mates

- You try to 'wah' your civvy mates and they think you're stupid because they don't understand the 'wah' concept!

- Someone points something out to you and your response is – 'SEEN' –

- You have not heard something someone says to you – instead of saying 'Pardon me, can you repeat that please?' you say 'Say again, Over'

- You wonder why the girl you have just failed miserably to bag off with slaps you in the face after you ask her if she thinks her fat mate would be up for it instead

- You hear someone farting (or fart yourself) and you immediately shout out loudly 'EASE SPRINGS'

- You refer to any form of activity as 'phys' –

- You can't stop saying "good drills" when someone does something u approve of...

- You 'Burst into Flames' when your civvy mates are having a cigarette

- You wear flip flops in to the shower, even at a Family member's house!

- Whenever you are involved in the organization of a private function you get everyone to form an extended line and make a sweep of the area to pick up any gash, you walking behind to make sure they keep in line and have not missed anything...

- Turds are no longer disgusting, they are a comedy prop

- You can't go shopping without having to go into Blacks and every Camping Shop and Army Surplus Store!

- You are able to turn an entire fridge's content into an 'All-In' feast for the family

- You have an unnatural ability to sleep anywhere and on anything!

- You insist on giving out full 'Actions On' for all possibilities to your Family before taking them to Tesco's shopping or for a days' outing!

- You get puzzled looks from your Kids when you ask them who threw the 'Admin Grenade' in their room

- You are unfamiliar with an area, you always insist on doing a quick recce

- You refer to the general public as "Effin civvies"...........even your parents

- You can fully understand any accent in the UK regardless of how thick the accent actually is

- You make your kids sew any pocket that they lost a button from, in three different colours of thread and you inspect afterwards to make sure they complied with your required '100 Stitches to the Inch' –

- You refuse outright to buy a tool set as your Leatherman can do everything a tool set can!

- You cringe, and mutter under your breath 'Get a shaggin haircut' when you see men with long hair

- You find running around in a big circle with 50 other people 'punching out to the front' normal

- Even though you have a perfectly working kettle in the house you insist on making a 'brew' on your hexamine cooker or Coleman gas stove out in the back garden

- You call all manner of sweets – 'Stickies' –

- You say to your civvy mates 'Tea, NATO, at the speed of a thousand gazelles – GO!' and you get annoyed when you have to explain what the hell you're on about

- To you a Strawberry Mivvie isn't an ice cream on a stick but is the term you use for anyone not in the Military

- You refer to a resident Falkland Islander as a 'Still'–

- Everyone who isn't a Squaddie or a mate you refer to as a PONTI (Person Of No Tactical Importance)

- You're late for a night out and your civvy mate rings you to find out where you are and you reply, 'Don't worry – ETA figures one zero', and he hasn't got a scooby what you're on about

- The word 'Freckles' has nothing to do with skin markings but has everything to do with a game you once played in the Squadron Bar!

- You can't understand your civvy mates when you get split up on a night out and they fail to go back to the last RV (and they don't understand when you tell them it is part of SOP's")

- You insist on using a lighter to remove threads from clothing even when there is a pair of scissors or sharp knife handy!

- You get dressed up in a suit for a posh do and still wear your G10 watch or a G Shock

- You have an uncanny ability to pack the entire contents of your house into eight MFO Boxes and in less than a day! You also manage to pack everything you need last – first and you hand write a list of contents for each Box, placing one list in each and keeping a copy yourself

- You insist that Harry Black – Masking Tape can fix anything

- You know what all your fellow/former Squaddie mates' wives/girlfriends breasts look like even though you've never met them..." ☺

- You understand the term: 'Shit rolls down hill' to be very true!

- The word 'Swamp' means something entirely different from the average location within the Everglades of Florida

- Your Wife/Girlfriend is highly trained in Field Hand Signals, especially the 'On Me' Signal (extremely handy whilst out shopping)

- Playing darts in the local, you start blaming non application of the marksmanship principles as a reason for being crap!

- All your clothes, plus your Wife's and Kids' clothes are neatly folded 9" x 9

- You tell your workmate to 'get their shit squared away'!

- The only way your other half can you get you off the bedroom floor after you have passed out from a night on the lash is to shout at the top of her voice – 'STAND TO'-

- You wouldn't dare polish a pair of boots without having both an 'On' and an 'Off' Brush

- You still always check your pockets are done up when 'preparing to move', and you'd check your pouches too (if you had any)

- You use Voice Procedure when sending a Text Message

- You see an international athlete bang out a marathon in sub 2 hours 10 minutes and then mutter "all well and good but he couldn't do it with weight on his back!

- You refer to everything you own as your 1157

- You have no problem reciting your Army Number but haven't the foggiest what your Mobile Phone number is!

- You insist on saying 'Mag to Grid' instead of 'Get Rid'-

- You still own Ron Hills and a moth-eaten Helly Hansen and wear them shopping!

- You use the word 'Endex' a lot!

- You pang for 'Range Stew' and a 'Brew' (in a 58 Pattern Mug of course)

- You watch a gun flick – you count the rounds fired and can't help but whisper 'mag change!'

- You believe The North Face, Cragghoppers, Berghaus, Ron Hill, Helly Hansen and Lowe Alpine are all top fashion designer wear and Millets is the very top of the range shop for up to date fashion clothing

- You go shopping with your mates the first Saturday of the month, spend the majority of your wages on expensive 'Designer Wear' walking clothing/gear, the latest GPS etc. and end up leaving it all behind in the last pub you visited during your after-shopping all-day session!

- Your four year old can stand to attention, about turn and salute. Correctly!!!

- You shout 'De-Bus' upon arrival at your destination in a minicab full of your muckers

- Whenever you are stopped in the street and asked directions to any location in town you can't help but give out full Grid coordinates and insist on writing a full route-card for the person/family asking directions

- You can't resist Shouting out "GAS! GAS! GAS!" whenever someone farts!

19. Epilogue

I hadn't expected to write an epilogue so early; maybe for a second edition, should that ever appear, but hardly before the book was first published. So what changed my mind? Well, during the production process a number of the stories were passed to friends and website acquaintances for comment. All were supportive and enthusiastic, and most were keen to get a hold of the finished article. I hope they haven't been disappointed! This one-page addition was prompted by their pre-publication interest.

So what? You might ask. Well, Bod had the answer in the first chapter when he referred to a cascade effect. Every other reply to the stories circulated contained the phrase "reminds me of the time...", and most offered to contribute stories of their own. The act of writing has also continued to spark the memory, and could have become an endless process had the decision not been taken to draw a line under the work so far.

You're probably already ahead of me. The logical conclusion is a sequel, and after pulling up a sandbag what can be more appropriate than adding a second sandbag for comfort?

Many thanks to all who have bought this book, and hence boosted support to a worthwhile charity. I sincerely hope that you have enjoyed reading it and that you have found at least one story worthy of telling in the years to come. If it was just the one, then look out for '**Another Sandbag**' and I'm sure you'll find one more!

Jonathan Smiles